BY
KELLOGG FOUNDATION

At
Ba

KRA
MTS.

COAST

LARSEN PEN.

C.Ann

ENDERBY
LAND

Edward VIII
Bay
KEMP COAST

Mawson

LARS
CHRISTENSEN
COAST

PRINCE CHARLES MTS.

MacKenzie
Bay

AMERICAN HIGHLAND

Four Ladies
Bank
VESTFOLD HILLS

INGRID
CHRISTENSEN
COAST

C A

MT. GAUSS

Davis
Sea

Mirny

90°

Pionerskaya

12

HASWELL
ISLETS

Shackleton
Ice Shelf

AXEL
HEIBERG
GLACIER

HORLICK

MAUD RANGE

3

SHACKLETON GLACIER
BEARDMORE GLACIER
MT. MARKHAM

Geomagnetic
Pole

BUNGER HILLS

KNOX
COAST

4

7

Ross
Ice
Shelf

Shackleton Inlet

MT. McCLINTOCK

FERRAR GLACIER

Vincennes
Bay

BUDD
COAST

ROOSEVELT I.
LITTLE AMERICA

1

Kainan
Bay

ROSS I.

EDWARD VII
PEN.

McMurdo Sd.

VICTORIA LAND

2

AREA OF
MAGNETIC
POLE

WILKES LAND

BANZARE COAST

120°

Ross Sea

5

ADELIE
LAND

COMMANDANT
CHARCOT GL.

POSSESSION
IS.

6

Pt. Géologie
Port Martin

Cape Adare

Cape
Freshfield

Cape Denison

Smith Inlet
Rennick Bay

NINNIS
GLACIER

MERTZ GLACIER

Indian
Ocean

BALLENY IS.

ANTARCTIC CIRCLE

150°

SCOTT I.

180°

L. Manditch

WHITE
LAND
OF
ADVENTURE

THE STORY OF THE ANTARCTIC

WHITE
LAND
OF
ADVENTURE

74921

THE STORY OF THE ANTARCTIC

WALTER SULLIVAN

Illustrated with maps and photographs

WHITTLESEY HOUSE

McGraw-Hill Book Company, Inc.

New York   Toronto   London

Published by Whittlesey House
A division of the McGraw-Hill Book Company, Inc.

ACKNOWLEDGMENTS

This book would never have come to pass without the tireless efforts of my wife, Mary. She helped edit the original book and was instrumental in preparing this abridged edition.

Special thanks must go to the U. S. Navy, which permitted me to accompany three Antarctic expeditions and meet a fourth for its homeward voyage, and to *The New York Times,* in whose service I did so. *The Times* has kindly permitted me to draw on material which I wrote for that newspaper and to use photographs taken in its behalf.

I am also particularly indebted to the late Rear Admiral Richard E. Byrd, who provided photographs and allowed me to quote extensively from his works. I received generous aid from many others, but space does not permit listing them all. The following were particularly helpful in furnishing exploration records, accounts, technical advice, and photographs and in giving permission to quote from personal diaries: Rear Admiral George J. Dufek, Rear Admiral Henry H. Caldwell, Dr. Paul A. Siple, Captain Richard B. Black, Captain John J. Hourihan, Prof. Richard F. Flint, James R. Balsley, the Scott Polar Research Institute in Cambridge, England, the Expéditions Polaires Françaises (Missions Paul-Émile Victor) in Paris and the Alexander Turnbull Library in New Zealand.

Walter Sullivan
Riverside, Connecticut

CONTENTS

1

The Ice Age in Being

A T THE BOTTOM of the world lies a mighty continent still wrapped in the Ice Age. It is almost as large as Europe and Australia combined, yet less than 1 per cent of its territory has been covered on foot by man.

For years the icy mysteries of Antarctica have drawn the adventurous. Hardy explorers have sailed through the pack ice to probe its coast. Three immortal men— Shackleton, Amundsen, and Scott—blazed the perilous trail to the South Pole itself. More recently airplanes have crisscrossed the continent's rugged interior, seeking to explore the unknown hinterland.

Now, although huge areas are still unknown to man, Antarctic exploration has taken on a new dimension. Hidden in the continent's icy crust and in the atmosphere above it are secrets of great interest to science. During the International Geophysical Year of 1957–1958 simultaneous scientific observations are being made all over the world to extend man's knowledge of the earth and the space through which it is flying. Antarctica is a chief focal point in this vast international program. Ten nations have set up scientific stations there to observe the magnetic forces and cosmic rays which can best be studied

9

near the Poles. Scientists are examining the ice itself—to see how deep it is, what lies beneath the continent's icy shroud, and whether it is shrinking.

Answers to questions of the most fundamental sort are being sought. As a result of the I.G.Y. we should know much more, not only of the Antarctic Continent, but of the rest of the world too.

Antarctica's past and future are of especial interest to young people, for to them it is the last great frontier on our planet. Many of its scientific secrets, as well as its yet unsighted mountains and glaciers, will be discovered by those who today are still in their teens.

Before we set out with the men who explored this icy wilderness let us first take a look at the nature of the land itself and the penguins, seals, and whales who frequent its coasts.

Antarctica differs fundamentally from the Arctic regions at the opposite end of the globe. The Arctic is an ocean, covered with drifting pack ice and hemmed in by the land masses of Europe, Asia, and North America. The Antarctic presents the reverse situation. It is a continent centered roughly on the South Pole and surrounded by the most unobstructed water areas of the world—the Atlantic, Pacific, and Indian Oceans.

The continental ice sheet is over two miles high in its center and refrigerates the air over the bottom of the earth far more than that over the Arctic. Thus more than a million persons live within 2,000 miles of the North Pole in an area that includes most of Alaska, Siberia, and Scandinavia, rich in forest and mining industries. Within the same distance of the South Pole there is not a single tree, industry, or settlement, apart from a handful of weather stations.

Presumably no place in the world is as cold as the mountain-ringed South Polar Plateau. Nearer the coast temperatures have been registered as low as —88°. In summer, on the other hand, when the sun shines brightly on a protected place, a man may strip to his waist. The seasons in Antarctica follow the pattern of the southern hemisphere. Summer begins in November and winter starts in June. The summer days and the winter nights become longer as one approaches the continent until, once the Antarctic Circle has been crossed, there is a period of continuous daylight in midsummer and of un-broken darkness in midwinter. If one keeps on moving toward the South Pole these periods lengthen until at the Pole itself there is only one "day" a year, with six months of daylight and six months of darkness.

Antarctica is a living example of what happened to much of North America and Europe shortly before the dawn of civilization. Like the ice sheets of the North which retreated, leaving such relics as the Great Lakes, the Antarctic ice has shrunk. It is at least 1,000 feet thinner than it was, and a few isolated valleys and strips of coastline have been laid bare. Nevertheless in the hinterland only the loftiest mountains pierce the blue and white crust which still blankets almost the entire continent.

Until the moon or other planets are attained, Antarctica will remain the most unearthly region within the reach of man. The landscape is so strange that special

11

words are needed to describe it. Nunataks, the tips of mountain peaks, poke their heads above the ice sheet. Winds, pressures, tensions of almost inexpressible violence mold the ice and the granular snow, or névé, into countless strange shapes—sastrugi, bergschrunds, barrancas, dongas, hummocks, séracs. Even volcanoes thrust their fiery heads through the Antarctic ice—how many no one knows.

The great mass of the continent is buried under a moving ice sheet. Just as other continents shed water Antarctica sheds ice. Snow falls on the ice sheet, adding constantly to its bulk, and then the ice flows, sometimes over 1,000 miles, to the sea. Rivers of fast-flowing ice, or glaciers, cut through the plains of more stagnant ice to the ocean.

The ice sheet does not pour into the sea at certain places only, as is the case with watersheds. It pushes out in virtually all directions. Icebergs break off, or "calve," from the ice front along almost the entire coastline.

Where the ice sheet has pushed out over the sea and is afloat, though still attached to the continent, it is known as an ice shelf. The largest example of it covers a mighty gulf on the Pacific coast of Antarctica. Known as the Ross Ice Shelf, it is roughly the size of France, with a seaward front of 400 miles. Such ice shelves produce the flat-topped icebergs typical of Antarctica—great wafers of ice about 700 feet thick and sometimes 100 miles long.

Though several thousand miles of Antarctic coastline have not been reached by ship, it is evident from what we have seen that much of the shore consists of ice cliffs some eighty feet above the water. Of all the sights that greet the newcomer to Antarctica, the uniformity of these ice cliffs is the most impressive.

The material from which the great Antarctic ice sheet has been built is the lowly snowflake. By wind action or compression the flakes become sandlike grains, and as they settle deeper under the weight of new snows they merge into larger and larger grains which finally congeal into true ice. Throughout the process the six-sided shape of the water molecule is reflected in the shape of the grains. They are invariably six-sided crystals. Frozen between them are bubbles of air which are compressed as the entire structure sinks deeper. If you make a tall drink with the deeper glacier ice, no soda is needed, for the air escaping as the ice melts is under pressure and effervesces.

In addition to the ice of the continent Antarctica produces "sea ice"—the material of which the "pack" is made. The pack is a belt of drifting ice which girdles Antarctica and kept the continent inviolate until the twentieth century. The pack is often 600 miles wide, but thins in some sectors and at some seasons to only twenty or thirty miles. Explorers have recently found that in a few places it may disappear altogether in late summer, allowing ships to sail right up to the ice- and rock-bound coasts.

Antarctica was once green with pine forests and jungles of tree-ferns, but today there is not a tree on the entire continent, and plants of any kind are so rare that explorers rejoice at finding even the lowliest moss or grass.

The most widespread of the plants are the lichens—scaly, paperlike plants that cling to the rocks even on mountains bordering the South Polar Plateau—the coldest place on earth. Some of the lichens found on Antarctic peaks, surrounded by hundreds of miles of barren ice sheet, display brilliant shades of red, yellow, and orange.

Over 300 kinds of lichen have been identified, sixty types of moss, and one or two species of coarse grass. As a rule there is no visible soil in Antarctica. It has been plowed into the sea by the glaciers or blown away by the furious winds.

The first clue that Antarctica was not always buried under an ice sheet was the discovery in the summer of 1892–1893 of what seemed to be part of a fossil pine tree on Seymour Island, near the tip of Palmer Peninsula. Sixteen years later Shackleton and two companions, picking their way up Beardmore Glacier toward the South Pole, likewise found a petrified pine log and extensive seams of low-grade coal. Thus it became known that, in the Carboniferous and Permian Periods, the heart of Antarctica, now covered by a dense ice sheet, was once carpeted with waving swamp forests of palm and fernlike trees.

Fossil remains from more recent periods have been found in the vicinity of Palmer Peninsula, which thrusts 800 miles toward South America from the Antarctic mainland. At Mount Flora on the tip of the peninsula, no less than sixty-one species of Jurassic vegetation have been discovered, including thirteen kinds of cone-bearing

14

tree. Mount Flora today is a barren hump of rock in a black and white landscape, but the imprints of leaves and hemlock-type pine branches in its stones paint a vivid picture of the rain forests which thrived there, dense with fig trees, laurel, beech, and sequoia. The tree rings in the petrified logs have been studied and indicate a climate with marked seasons of heat and cold. During Jurassic times the world was dominated by the dinosaurs, but it seems probable that the forests, at least on Palmer Peninsula, continued up to the period when mammals and other modern animals began to emerge.

Who trod the dark jungles of Antarctica? So far no remains have been found of true land animals, though five types of prehistoric penguin have been discovered in the Palmer Peninsula area. Because of the continent's isolation, separated from its nearest neighbor, South America, by 600 miles of stormy seas, there may never have been four-footed creatures there. Nearby New Zealand, for example, has no native land mammals.

Antarctica presents many unsolved problems of the most fundamental sort. The Permian trees and plants found on the plateau near the South Pole are almost identical with those in the Permian deposits of South Africa, Australia, India, and South America. There have been various explanations for such close resemblance between such widely separated areas. Probably the most popular belief of today is that land bridges and island chains bridged the gaps, following submarine ridges such as those which still connect Antarctica with South America, Australia, and New Zealand. Another explanation is based on the theory that the continents in question drifted apart.

Antarctica seems to have been a bridge—if not the starting point—for wholesale plant migrations. In the mid-nineteenth century Charles Darwin, while working on his theory of evolution, found a great gap in the development of plant life and suspected that there may have been a remote region where the higher plants developed in isolation until they suddenly found a highway by which to reach the rest of the world.

"Nothing is more extraordinary in the history of the Vegetable Kingdom, as it seems to me," he wrote, "than the *apparently* very sudden or abrupt development of the higher plants. I have sometimes speculated whether there did not exist somewhere during long ages an extremely isolated continent, perhaps near the South Pole."

A century later we still cannot say whether, as Darwin suggested, the higher plants first evolved in Antarctica, but the view is widely accepted that that continent at least served as a migration route between South America and Australia.

What does the future hold? Will parts of Antarctica become more habitable in the foreseeable future? These are questions which cannot be answered until we know more of Antarctica's past. One of the tasks of the International Geophysical Year will be to feel the pulse of the earth's climatic changes and determine if the Antarctic ice sheet is in advance or retreat. In earlier stages of the earth's history the great periods of glaciation brought about radical changes in the development of the animal kingdom. Had it not been for the Ice Ages of the Permocarboniferous Period some scientists believe gigantic insects might have dominated the world. The cooling of the Cretaceous and Eocene Periods struck the death blow to the hordes of huge reptiles which roamed the earth and made way for the rise of the mammals. Finally the repeated glaciation of the Pleistocene created upheavals in the world of mammals and aided in the rise of the most intelligent and adaptable of that class of vertebrates—man.

These great changes, accompanied by marked variations in sea level, took place over many thousands of years, but only a slight modification in climate and ice conditions would be sufficient to make the coasts of Antarctica more accessible and bring its hidden—and as yet unknown—mineral resources within reach of the rest of the world.

2

Life on the Fringes

THE PACK is the focal point of life in Antarctica, for here is "earth's richest pasture," providing the plant food which is absent on the mainland. So cold are the waters in the pack that a man without waterproof clothing becomes unconscious within ten minutes and dies soon thereafter. Yet so dense is this water with tiny living creatures that it resembles murky soup. The opaqueness is due to plankton—a drifting cloud of little one-celled plants and tiny animals that feed on them. There is said to be more living matter per acre in these waters than anywhere on the globe, either on sea or land. When the sea freezes, layers of this plant life are caught in the ice but thrive there.

Bathed with sunlight filtering down through the ice, these one-celled plants perform the mysterious function of photosynthesis—the combining of carbon dioxide and water to form carbohydrates—upon which the lives of all animals depend. The plants in the sea are eaten by tiny creatures, who in turn are swallowed by larger fish, by great ninety-pound jellyfish, and by birds and mammals.

Even the largest of all animals, the blue whale, depends for its food on the little shrimplike krill of Antarctic

18

waters. The blue whale is, in fact, greater in bulk than anything which is known to have lived on the earth, the weight of the adult being roughly 150 tons.

The chief enemies of these giants are the killer whales, the "wolves of the sea" who hunt in packs and are the most vicious and sinister of the animals in Antarctica. They run to thirty feet in length and are easily recognized by a tremendous, sharklike dorsal fin which rises about five feet out of the water as they break the surface.

In the pack they swim under the ice in groups of from two to forty and when they sight a shadow overhead they know it means a potential dinner. They swim deep, developing tremendous momentum, and strike the ice with their backs, shattering it and spilling their prey into the water to be torn apart. They then stick their lizard-like heads six or eight feet out of the water, hanging there for a few moments while they look around on the ice for more seals or penguins.

The pack abounds in seals, most numerous of which are the crabeaters, one of the least known of all mammals. Less than half a dozen crabeater pups have been seen, in all cases on the drifting floes of the pack. The crabeater's teeth have developed into a sieve through which he can eject sea water, straining out the shrimp that form the bulk of his diet.

Only one animal lives on the coastal ice of the Antarctic, independent of the pack. That is the Weddell seal who, like the Emperor penguin, is remarkably adapted for life in an Ice Age. His range is farther south than that of any mammal except man himself.

19

The Weddell seal is considerably bigger, even, than the crabeater, for he may weigh 900 pounds and is roughly 10 feet long from nose to flipper. His life centers on the ice which covers the bays and inlets along the coast, especially where pressure has wrinkled the sea ice into ridges, creating havens out of the wind and lines of weakness in the ice where the seals can bore air holes. Their teeth are especially adapted for this purpose, the hole being sawed by a circular motion of the jaw.

This enables them to take refuge from the terribly low temperatures that descend on the coast during the winter night. The water under the ice never gets below 28° above zero, whereas the air above drops to 75° below zero. By keeping their breathing holes open the seals can stay under the ice almost constantly. Their colonies may be five miles or more from open water.

The seals have a mysterious device for locating blow holes, even in the stygian midwinter darkness under the snow-covered ice. It is not a question of memory, for if a man chops a new hole a seal is likely to poke his nose out shortly thereafter. They rarely seem to hold their breath more than fifteen minutes, yet they set off in pursuit of fish and squid, which they track down and devour in the black depths, and find their way back to a hole within that time limit.

The bulls apparently fight savage underwater battles during the rutting season and emerge at that time covered with wounds. Eleven months later, in the early spring, the female crawls out on the ice to give birth to her pup, a snug roll of fuzz about fifty-seven inches long.

She nurses the baby for a month, producing tremendous quantities of milk, for the pup gains about seven pounds a day.

Some animals seek seclusion when injured or ill, but some Antarctic seals carry this to unbelievable extremes. On the sledge journeys made by Scott's men from McMurdo Sound they found dead or dying seals as much as forty miles inland and 2,400 feet above sea level, far from any source of food.

Rivaling the killer whale as the villain of Antarctica is the sea leopard. He is a member of the seal family but, unlike his fat cousins, he is predatory, with a head like that of a gigantic serpent and an elongated neck. Although slow and clumsy on ice, his body, a ten-foot ribbon of muscle, is menacingly swift in the water. Not only is he a nimble swimmer but he has been seen to leap out and snatch penguins who were standing too close to the edge of a floe.

The birds of Antarctica have helped man in many ways during his perilous journeys into the pack. They have fed him, guided him, and the blubbery penguins have even provided emergency fuel for his steamships. The mariner who sees shags in a fog knows that danger is near, for those birds—a form of cormorant—rarely fly more than a few miles from the rocks where they live. The sighting of snow petrels, on the other hand, is often the first warning that ice is close by. This is one of the most beautiful of all birds, resembling in flight a form of white swallow.

The vultures of the Antarctic are the skua gulls. They

prey heavily on the Adélie penguin rookeries, swooping in to snatch the unprotected chicks. Most remarkable of all, the skua penetrates to the barren heart of Antarctica. Of the four parties of men who have climbed to the 10,000-foot plateau near the South Pole all but one saw skua gulls, though they were as much as 600 miles from the nearest source of food.

The most characteristic creatures of Antarctica are the penguins. The Adélie penguin and Emperor penguin, like the Antarctic skua, are found nowhere else. The Adélie stands about two feet high and most closely resembles the cartoonist's concept of the penguin. He is the clown of Antarctica. The Emperor penguin is as dignified in stature and demeanor as his name implies. He is perhaps the most remarkable animal relic of the Ice Age and is regarded by some, in terms of evolution, as the most primitive of all birds. Both species are excellent swimmers. Their wings have become flippers and they "fly" under water with sufficient speed to catch fish. The Adélies can dive into the water from a height of twelve feet and can leap onto ice floes five feet high. This they do by swimming deep and soaring out of the water at great speed, landing feet first on the ice. In groups they assume echelon formation so that they plop down on the ice in quick succession, side by side. They are devoured by curiosity and, like most Antarctic creatures, are so wild that they are tame, for they have no natural enemies on the ice and when they see a man will waddle eagerly over to have a better look. When pursued on foot they cannot run fast but can easily outdistance their pursuers by falling on their bellies and tobogganing away over the snow, propelled by their web feet and their flipperlike wings.

In the spring the Adélie migrates from the pack and begins building his nest at one of the rock-strewn rookery sites. The nest is made of small stones and pebbles collected by the male as part of the courtship. The male comes up to the nest where his spouse is standing, bows low before her and then drops the stone at her feet. This is repeated over and over for many days.

Once the chicks have been born they get their food by poking their heads down their parents' throats and eating regurgitated krill. At the rookery on Cape Adare this keeps the adults continually on the go as many of the nests are over 1,000 feet above the water. The little birds have to use feet, bill, and flippers to scramble up the long rocky path from the sea to the rookery, as high above the water as the summit of the Empire State Building.

The Adélies lay two eggs a season but the mortality is heavy—over 68 percent in some cases—the weaker chicks being carried off by the skuas. There are believed to be as many as a million Adélies in some of the larger rookeries. The sight of one of these great multitudes of birds in their white waistcoats and black jackets is a reminder that the Antarctic mainland is one of the few areas in the world where animal life is still in its virgin state of abundance, unaffected by the depredations of man.

The Emperor penguin is one of the largest birds, for he weighs close to ninety pounds and stands three feet tall. He commutes in the opposite directions from the

Adélie and all "normal" birds, for in the fall he heads south toward the Pole and the coldest weather, laying and hatching his single egg on ice during the winter night before heading north again into the pack and a less frigid climate.

The Emperor is the bird who most completely adjusted his life cycle to the conditions which exterminated all inhabitants of once-verdant Antarctica except those capable of adapting themselves to life on ice and in the water. The hatching of his egg on ice is probably a trick he learned during the period when Antarctica was so completely buried that the land areas used as rookeries by the Adélies and other species were all covered. The Emperor broods his egg in a snug corner between the tops of his feet and the rolls of fat on his lower abdomen. There is logic to his hatching his one chick during the winter night, for only thus is there time to rear the youngster to the point where he is self-sufficient for the next winter.

When still small the chicks are completely concealed inside the pocket of loose flesh under the adult's abdomen, but when hungry—which is often—they stick out their scrawny heads and whistle in a raucous manner. Dr. Edward Wilson of the Scott expeditions tried to raise two of the chicks and found that these whistles of hunger were ear-splitting. At least three times every night he was roused from his slumber and had to chew seal meat to feed to the penguin babies, both of whom nevertheless died within a few weeks.

When it came time for the birds of the rookery to return to their summer home in the pack, Wilson found that they had free transportation. Every day when there was a brisk south wind a contingent of birds would gather on the seaward edge of a nearby patch of frozen ocean. Before long this section of ice would break off and blow north toward the pack beyond the horizon. The big birds were like orderly passengers during the rush hour, with about 100 at a time marching out single file to wait for the next floe going north.

The only land animals in Antarctica are a few species of insect who eke out their existence among the rocks and mountains in the hinterland, in the penguin rookeries, or in the small rivulets of melt-water that run down rocky slopes here and there on the coast. The winds are so furious that the spiders spin no webs and the flies are wingless. These species spend almost their entire lives frozen solid. They thaw out for a few days each year and hurriedly carry out their life processes in order to keep the species going.

3

The First Discoveries

WHEN WAS ANTARCTICA first discovered? Until the world was well into the nineteenth century it lay beyond man's ken. The snows sifted down, the blizzards screamed, millions of penguins, seals, and whales migrated to and from their breeding grounds as they had since before the dawn of civilization. But of this man knew nothing, although some suspected the existence of a land mass capping the bottom of the globe.

As the early explorers reached farther into the South Pacific they discovered lush, inhabited lands which they took to be portions of this "Southern Continent." These later proved to be islands, and in 1772 Captain James Cook, one of the greatest of all explorers, circled the drifting ice fields surrounding Antarctica. It was obvious to him that if any continent existed it lay south of this ice and was an utterly desolate land.

This was enough to dampen the enthusiasm of explorers for many years to come. It was not until the turn of the nineteenth century, when the seal and sea elephant population of more northerly lands was exterminated, that men looked toward the icy south with revived interest.

It was this southward advance by sealers that probably led to the first sighting of Antarctica, although it is possible that the mainland was seen earlier by some ship driven south while rounding Cape Horn. The question of who first saw the continent has become a controversial one. The Americans, British, and Russians all claim the honor, the dates of their alleged first sightings falling within the span of a single year.

In the official American view, as set forth in the U.S. Navy Sailing Directions that describe that region, the discoverer was Nathaniel Palmer, who at an age of less than twenty-one commanded the sealing sloop *Hero* out of Stonington, Connecticut. During the southern summer of 1820–1821 the *Hero* and four other Stonington ships operated out of an extraordinary harbor which they had discovered among islands near the Antarctic mainland. It was the crater of an extinct volcano which had ruptured and allowed the sea to enter, forming a snug, circular harbor. The ring of land surrounding the bay is now known as Deception Island.

On November 17, 1820, Palmer sailed south in search of seals and described in his log the discovery of an ice-clogged strait, probably Orleans Channel, one side of which was the mainland.

Several months later Palmer made another exploratory excursion to the southeast, on which he is believed to have discovered the large and mountainous islands now known as the Palmer Archipelago. On his way back he was fog-bound and becalmed. When the mist began thinning he found himself between two large men-of-war. He broke

27

the Stars and Stripes from his masthead and the warships hoisted the Cross of St. Andrew—the flag of Imperial Russia. It was the expedition led by Admiral Thaddeus von Bellingshausen.

The Russians were astounded to see so tiny a craft in this forbidding region. They had thought themselves the first to penetrate these waters, but, as recorded in Bellingshausen's own log, when Palmer was invited aboard the flagship he told the admiral that he had been operating in this area for four months.

The British contender as first man to see Antarctica was Edward Bransfield, aboard the brig *Williams*. In October, 1819, while carrying cargo around Cape Horn, the *Williams* under the command of William Smith detoured south and found a series of bleak islands, now known as the South Shetlands. Here, according to his report, he landed "and took formal possession of the new discovered land in the Name of His Majesty George the Third."

When he reached Valparaiso, Smith reported his action to British naval officers there. The British officers saw in this discovery an opportunity to obtain a foothold on the south side of the sea passage linking the Atlantic and Pacific—a most valuable asset in those days of rival empire-building. They chartered the *Williams*, hired Smith as pilot and placed Edward Bransfield of the Royal Navy in command.

The ship entered the great sound now known as Bransfield Strait, bounded on one side by Palmer Peninsula and on the other by the South Shetland Islands. The

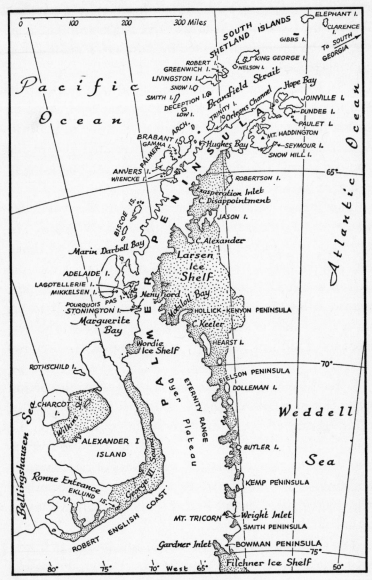

Palmer Peninsula

weather was intermittently foggy; hence they did not see the mainland side of the strait until, on January 30, 1820, the air cleared somewhat and they sighted land to the southwest as well as islands to the east and northeast. The official American view is that this land was not Palmer Peninsula, but Trinity Island, which lies several miles offshore.

The contender of the Russians as first man to see Antarctica was a most uncontentious naval officer named Bellingshausen. After Napoleon's disastrous retreat from Moscow, Russia had emerged as a world power. Expeditions were sent to learn more about the polar regions at both the top and bottom of the globe. Bellingshausen, with two naval vessels, the corvettes *Vostok* and *Mirny,* was sent south and became the first man to circumnavigate Antarctica since Cook's voyage. He was a cautious explorer and not until his second season, in January, 1821, did he claim a sighting of land. On the outer edge of the ice pack he saw ice-capped rock cliffs rising several thousand feet from the sea. This he named Peter I Island for the great czar who was the father of Russian exploration and who had sent Bering forth to discover much of Alaska.

Six days later, on January 28, the Russians sighted a rugged mountainous coast which they named Alexander I Land in honor of the then czar of Russia. For over a century it was thought to be part of the mainland and thus was the chief foundation for the Russian argument that Bellingshausen was discoverer of the continent. Not until the memorable sledge journey in 1940 of the Americans Finn Ronne and Carl Eklund was it proved to be an island.

For the next fifteen years the chief stimulus to Antarctic exploration continued to be the quest for new sealing grounds.

The best-known figure of this generation was the Scotsman James Weddell, who reported that in February, 1823, he sailed south in a vast ice-free sea to the east of Palmer Peninsula, reaching Latitude 74°15′ South. The region is known today as the Weddell Sea, and the large seals which the Scotsman described also bear his name.

Much of the most important exploration of this decade was sponsored by Enderby Brothers, a whaling and sealing firm in London. Some of the grimmest pages in maritime history tell of the long voyages made by the little ships sent forth by this firm. Off what is now known as Enderby Land the crews of the *Tula* and *Lively* were almost annihilated by scurvy, the latter crew reaching port with only the captain, one seaman, and a cabin boy alive. The *Rose* was crushed in the ice north of the Weddell Sea, the first known victim of the Antarctic pack. Her companion vessel, *Hopeful,* rescued the crew, but the men on the *Sabrina* a few years later were not so fortunate. They and their ship vanished forever in a storm.

These disasters underlined the growing realization in the ports of England and New England that the meager residue of fur-bearing seals in the Antarctic no longer justified the perils of hunting them down. Ventures into the Antarctic might have stopped altogether had not a new interest been awakened.

Modern science was coming into being, and one of its most ardent protagonists was Alexander von Humboldt, a German scientist, explorer, and natural philosopher. One of his special fields of interest was the magnetic force that controls a compass needle. It was known that this "terrestrial magnetism" varied in direction and in intensity with changes in time and place. It was suspected by some that these variations were universal rather than local in nature.

Humboldt persuaded the czar to set up magnetic observatories across Russia until the line of stations reached from Europe to Peking. It soon became apparent that fluctuations in the earth's magnetism take place simultaneously all over the world.

It remained for another German, Johann Karl Friedrich Gauss, to devise a formula relating the three elements of the earth's magnetic force—its horizontal direction, its vertical direction, and its intensity—in terms of any point on the surface of the globe. This led to the supposition that there must be a South Magnetic Pole opposite the North Magnetic Pole. Achievement of the South Magnetic Pole would help confirm and expand the new theories.

There ensued three government expeditions—British, French, and American—which headed for Antarctica within two years of one another.

The French expedition, under Dumont D'Urville, sailed from Tasmania with two ships on New Year's Day, 1840, and headed southeast in the direction of the Magnetic Pole. On January 21 their "dip needle" showed that the direction of the magnetic force was only 4° from vertical, and their compasses were spinning wildly, indicating their nearness to the Pole, but an ice-covered coast barred the way. A party rowed to a string of islets which lay a few hundred yards off shore and proclaimed the land French soil. D'Urville called the region Adélie Land for his wife.

A week after leaving this spot, while threading their way through fog-shrouded icebergs, the two French ships sighted a brig coming toward them flying the Stars and Stripes. It was the American ship *Porpoise* of the squadron commanded by Lieutenant Charles Wilkes.

Wilkes had set forth with four naval vessels: the sloops-of-war *Vincennes* and *Peacock,* the gun-brig *Porpoise,* and the supply ship *Relief,* plus two New York pilot boats, *Sea Gull* and *Flying Fish.*

It was not only the largest expedition to venture into the Antarctic up until that time, but its two sloops-of-war were probably the biggest ships to do so before the days of steam. Nevertheless the expedition and its men were poorly prepared for polar exploration, both in clothing and equipment, and the ships themselves were in some cases badly rotted.

A year and a half after leaving the United States, Wilkes' flagship *Vincennes* reached pack ice near the sector where the Magnetic Pole was presumed to lie. One of his ships, the *Sea Gull,* had vanished with all hands in a gale off Cape Horn, and the others disappeared for weeks at a time in the stormy seas.

At last, on January 30, they reached a bay ringed with

rocks and a wall of ice. This was either the very spot where the French had landed nine days before, or close to it. Wilkes named it Piner Bay for his signal quartermaster. On the basis of his magnetic observations here and elsewhere along the coast he estimated that the Magnetic Pole lay about 230 miles inland due south of this point.

For over two weeks Wilkes continued to work westward. Several times he saw land and by now was certain that he was sailing along a continental coastline—not past scattered islands. If he could only sail west far enough he could prove that the coast tied up with Enderby Land, discovered by one of the Enderby ships nine years earlier 2,500 miles west of Piner Bay.

After covering half that distance, on February 16, he met an ice wall directly across his path. He had no recourse but to turn north, naming the obstacle Termination Land. We know now it was a peninsula of continental ice jutting over 100 miles out from the coast and later named Shackleton Ice Shelf.

When Wilkes returned to the United States, instead of receiving a hero's welcome he was court-martialed, accused by his own officers of oppression, injustice, and misconduct of various sorts. Of the 585 crewmen engaged for the expedition, 127 had deserted and another 23 had died or been killed by native islanders. Wilkes appears to have been an irascible and stern officer, but his stubbornness led him to the consecutive land sightings which suggested the outline of a continent symmetrically capping the bottom of the earth.

The British expedition, led by James Clark Ross, set forth one year after Wilkes and two years after D'Urville, somewhat piqued that the others had already sailed to the vicinity of the Magnetic Pole. Although the Englishman's two vessels were less than half the size of Wilkes' flagship, they were specially reinforced to operate in pack ice. Thus for the first time it was possible for an Antarctic explorer to plunge boldly into the pack to see what lay on the far side of that belt of drifting floes.

On January 5, 1841, Ross entered the pack not far from the International Date Line and, to his utter amazement, after four days his ships broke out into an open sea. Not a speck of ice was to be seen anywhere. The sea extended unimpeded for 500 miles to the southeast.

Steaming south across what today is known as the Ross Sea, Ross and his men sighted a mountain-studded coastline which curved and ran almost due south at a point they named Cape Adare. A landing on the mainland was blocked by drift ice that hugged the shore, but they ran their boats onto the rocky beach of a small island and claimed the entire region for their young queen. In her honor Ross named it Victoria Land.

They sailed several hundred miles south along the coast until their compasses showed they had passed the position of the Pole, which lay inland. The mountains became ever higher, and at length they saw, reaching into the sky, an immense mass of snow from whose summit clouds of steam were belching forth. At night flames within the mountain were reflected on the vapor clouds above it. They gazed in wonder at the incredible sight of a volcano thrusting its head through Antarctic ice. It was later determined to be 13,200 feet high—one of the loftier volcanoes of the world. Near it was a sister peak, also of volcanic shape. They were named Erebus and Terror for the two ships of the expedition.

To the right was a deep indentation which Ross called McMurdo Bay, not realizing that the volcanic mountains stood on an island linked to the mainland only by an ice shelf. The "bay" is now charted as a sound and, with the Bay of Whales, which Ross discovered the next year, has been one of the two most important centers of Antarctic exploration.

Ross could no longer sail south, for the way was blocked by an even wall of ice, which he followed for hundreds of miles to the east, and which today is known as the Ross Ice Shelf. It is an immense expanse of ice, generally afloat, about 700 feet thick, filling a gulf roughly the size of France in the mountain-lined coast of Antarctica.

4

The Winter Night

STRANGE TO SAY, although the memorable voyages of Ross opened the door to an entire sector of the continent, fifty-two years elapsed before the next ship sailed through it. The world almost forgot about Antarctica, and it was not until the close of the nineteenth century that a new series of scientific expeditions was launched. The first, organized by Belgium, gave the world its initial glimpse into the mysterious darkness of the Antarctic night, for the expedition ship was trapped in the ice.

The Belgians set forth from Antwerp in 1897 in a Norwegian sealer which they renamed *Belgica*. After exploring along the west coast of Palmer Peninsula the ship skirted the ice to the southwest and ventured deep into a lead of open water that ran southward. Suddenly a shift in wind caused the ice floes to flow together, trapping the ship. For a full year the *Belgica* drifted, a prisoner. Those aboard her became the first to endure the winter night of Antarctica.

The *Belgica* appeared to be motionless, for the fields of ice in which she was locked moved in unison. It was only by observation of the stars that her constant movement became apparent. In the first two months alone she zigzagged a distance of 500 miles, penetrating involuntarily a region never before seen. The scientists, who cut holes in the ice to fish for marine life, also took frequent soundings of the depth of the water. Whenever the ship drifted southward the water became shallower. The whims of wind and current appeared to be carrying them back and forth across the rim of a continental shelf and they became convinced that not far to the south there was land.

As the nights grew longer there was no hope that they would be able to escape before total darkness fell. They roofed over the deck of the little 250-ton ship so they could move about with some shelter from winter gales.

Two men who later won fame—or ill-fame—in the polar regions were among the eighteen on the *Belgica*. They were the Norwegian Roald Amundsen, who served as first mate, and Dr. Frederick A. Cook, who was the ship's surgeon. Amundsen later conquered the South Pole and Cook claimed to have been first to the North Pole, although he was later accused of fraud and spent several years in jail. There is nothing in the accounts of the *Belgica* expedition to suggest dishonesty on his part at that time and Amundsen described him, among all those on board, as "the one man of unfaltering courage, unfailing hope, endless cheerfulness and universal kindness."

As the night dragged on the ship's captain, Georges Lecointe, collapsed, an apparent victim of malnutrition. Cook's treatment for the captain and others in a similar condition was a diet of fresh seal and penguin meat plus exposure to intensive heat from the stove. The latter, he hoped, would furnish a substitute for sunlight. The captain was the first man on whom he tried this, and within a week the patient was on his feet. According to Amundsen, it was Cook's insistence that they eat fresh seal meat which saved them all from succumbing to what was clearly scurvy.

Sick minds were an equally serious problem. Lethargy was universal. Even keeping up the log became a supreme effort. "We were never hungry, always tired, and the spirit never moved us," said Cook.

They sought to counter this lassitude by walking a circular path on the ice around the ship which came to be known as "madhouse promenade." Indeed the symptoms of insanity soon began to appear. One sailor, diagnosed by Cook as having become paranoiac, believed his shipmates sought to kill him and, when he slept, crawled into a tight corner of the ship. Another was seized by a form of hysteria that deprived him of both speech and hearing. "Only the return of the sun," said de Gerlache, the expedition leader, "saved him from madness."

After seventy-one days of continuous darkness the sun first appeared, briefly, on July 22. All hands climbed to various vantage points on the mast and on a nearby iceberg to welcome its return. "For several minutes my companions did not speak . . . ," said Cook. "Lecointe and Amundsen were standing on an iceberg close to me. They faced the light, and watched the fragment of the sun slide under the bergs, over hummocks, and along the even expanse of the frozen sea, with a worshipful air."

The new light shone on faces that were drawn and of a "sickly, jaundiced color, green and yellow and muddy," but their spirits suddenly soared with the sun; their strength returned. Yet as the weeks passed they realized that there was no assurance that they would escape the pack during the new summer season. Midsummer passed and they were still locked in the grip of a large floe, even though open water leads appeared here and there in the distance.

They decided to cut a canal to freedom. Week after week all hands manned the saws eight hours a day. Through ice up to seven feet thick they cut a canal 2,200 feet long and were within 100 feet of the ship when a wind shift closed the canal and wiped out their work. Two weeks later, on February 14, 1899, another wind shift opened up the canal and the ship steamed out of its prison.

As the *Belgica* returned to civilization, three other scientific expeditions were being prepared in Britain, Germany, and Sweden. All three sailed south in 1901 and two soon suffered a fate similar to that of the *Belgica*. The German expedition, led by Professor Dr. Erich von Drygalski, headed south in the *Gauss* along the meridian of 90° East in an effort to see if land lay between the sightings of Wilkes and Kemp (one of the Enderby captains). Just as the Germans thought they saw land the ship was locked in the ice fields and had to spend the winter there. Nevertheless the Germans sledged south over the floes and reached an extinct volcano which they named Mount Gauss for their ship. The next summer a pathway of ashes was laid on the ice from the ship to the nearest patch of open water. This absorbed enough sun heat to melt a trench six feet deep and ultimately became the line of cleavage, enabling the ship to escape. With the coal virtually exhausted, it was necessary to burn blubber-coated penguin bodies as fuel.

The Swedish expedition suffered a series of disasters. Under the leadership of Otto Nordenskjöld it headed for the Weddell Sea in the *Antarctic,* a former Norwegian whaler. Nordenskjöld and five others were landed at Snow Hill Island off the east coast of Palmer Peninsula with sufficient supplies for one winter, the plan being for the *Antarctic* to return for them the next season.

When summer came the ship failed to arrive, and the men prepared to spend another winter on the desolate and rocky shores of Snow Hill Island, slaughtering seals and penguins in great numbers for food and fuel.

Unable because of ice conditions to reach Snow Hill Island, the *Antarctic,* meanwhile, had landed three men at Hope Bay on the tip of Palmer Peninsula to try to sledge across the sound to the beleaguered winter party while the ship tried to reach the island by another route. The rescue party found there was no safe route across the sea ice and had to trudge back to Hope Bay. The *Antarctic* never returned for them.

As the days became longer the terrible truth became apparent. The trio would have to winter on that barren shore despite their lack of provisions or shelter. The robust Swedes were not easily disheartened. They built walls of stone and roofed them with their tent cloth.

Shoes, clothes, and fishing lines were fashioned from seals and penguins. Hooks were made from belt buckles and fish were caught for food.

When spring came, the "rescue party" started out again, coated with greasy soot from the blubber fire that had kept them alive. This time they found a solid route across the ice and rejoined the main party at Snow Hill Island.

The two groups were certain that some disaster had befallen the *Antarctic*. Their fears proved justified. After leaving Hope Bay, the ship had become "beset," that is, locked in the grip of the ice floes. The pressure in the pack, as it was driven against nearby islands, crushed her between the ice fields and she sank. The twenty men left on the ice managed to reach land on Paulet Island, some twenty-five miles away, where they built a hut and spent the winter. When summer came, several members of the party set forth in an open boat for Snow Hill Island. There they found that an Argentine ship dispatched to look for them had arrived that very day.

The purchase of provisions for this relief ship had been made by a young Englishman named Ernest Shackleton. When the Argentine ship picked up the remainder of the Swedish expedition at Paulet Island it deposited a large pile of stores at that point for any future victims of the Weddell Sea pack.

By one of the strange coincidences of polar exploration the next man to be cast away upon the floes of that treacherous sea was Shackleton himself. The Swedish expedition, despite its disaster, brought back valuable fossil specimens as well as much new geographical knowledge, but above all it had demonstrated that men cast away on the ice floes or left with meager provisions on the barren Antarctic coast could survive through ingenuity and fortitude if enough seals and penguins were available.

5

Into the Hinterland

WHILE the Swedes were fighting for survival in the Weddell Sea, Britain sent an expedition to the opposite side of Antarctica which marked the full-fledged emergence of the "Heroic Era" in Antarctic exploration. Born in the twilight of Victoria's reign, when Britain's empire had reached its prime, and lasting up to World War I, it is inseparably linked with the name of Robert Falcon Scott.

Scott led two expeditions to Antarctica, the second of which is by far the better known, for it culminated in his tragic race to the Pole. His first expedition was nevertheless the more important from the exploratory point of view because, for the first time, it reached into the interior of the continent. The coast, by now, had been seen at a number of points.

Scott and his men sailed from England in August, 1901, in a specially built ship, the *Discovery*. He selected McMurdo Sound for his base and set up his camp at Hut Point, a low rocky promontory at the southwest corner of Ross Island, almost in the smoking shadow of Mount Erebus.

When spring came, preparations were made for a long march south over the ice shelf at the southern edge of the

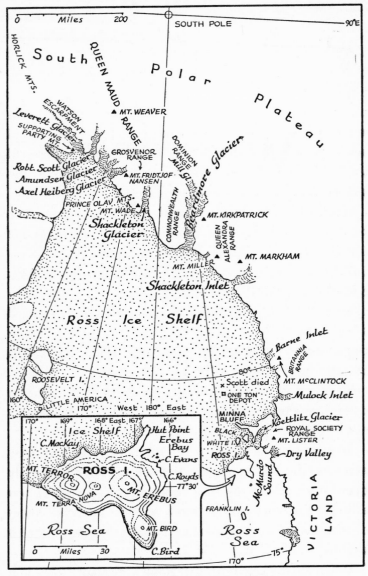

Routes to the South Polar Plateau

45

sound. From high ground Scott's party could see that
the mountains which lined the coast continued southward as far as the limit of their vision, flanked on the east
by a low expanse of ice shelf. It was therefore evident
that the true coast extended toward the South Pole, and
that the ice shelf over which they intended to travel was
a permanent ice blanket over the sea. Did the shelf reach
all the way to the Pole? Scott, Shackleton, and Dr. Edward A. Wilson started out with dogteams on November
2, 1902, to press as far south as possible.

After seven weeks on the march their route drew nearer
to the mountainous shoreline which they had been skirting and a magnificent panorama came into view. Slope
upon slope of snow rose ever higher until they saw a
magnificent twin summit over which hung a few strips
of cirrus cloud. They named it Mount Markham and,
at 15,100 feet, it is officially the highest known peak on
the Antarctic Continent, although some have been
sighted which may be loftier.

The line of mountains still ran on to the south, but
they knew they could not go much farther. At last, 380
miles from their ship, the three men turned back.

Wilson, a surgeon, examined his companions regularly
and soon noticed the ominous, plum-colored sores on
their gums and their feet. They began to complain of
stiff joints. Shackleton was the hardest hit, and Wilson
confided to Scott that their companion was badly stricken
with scurvy. They had allocated too little food for the
journey and hunger was their constant companion.

As an added blow their dogs died off rapidly until

finally all nineteen had perished. Scott and Wilson, despite their scurvy sores, had to do all the pulling. Shackleton picked his faltering way on skis. His fiery spirit would not admit defeat, but at last, after a prolonged period of coughing and gasping for breath, his spirits sagged. For considerable distances they had to haul him on a sledge. Had it not been for following winds from the south, which enabled them to rig the tent floor as a sledge sail, they might all have perished. On reaching McMurdo, after a homeward trek of over a month, they found that a relief ship, the *Morning*, had arrived and Shackleton could be sent home.

During Scott's absence a party under Lieutenant Armitage of the Royal Navy, second in command of the expedition, assaulted the wall of mountains that barred the way to the hinterland across the sound from their camp. They selected as their route an ice river that seemed to provide a smooth highway to the lofty interior. This Scott later named Ferrar Glacier for the expedition geologist. As they marched inland, the glacier rose ever higher until it overtopped the lesser mountains, and at last, on January 3, 1903, they saw nothing but a level snow-covered plateau ahead, as far as their range of vision. It was the first time that human eyes had gazed upon this plateau, which covers most of the interior of Antarctica. A few miles farther on they reached their highest point on the plateau—9,000 feet.

The next season Scott himself led a party up the Ferrar Glacier. At the summit he and two others struck out across the plateau. For seventeen days they marched west

47

toward the heart of the hinterland. When they turned back, after penetrating 200 miles from the top of the glacier, they had encountered absolutely no modification in scenery. Not a mountain, nor a hill, nor any appreciable change in the surface had been seen, except the varying patterns of sastrugi—the wind-carved furrows in the snow.

In descending the glacier on their return trip they digressed briefly to examine what seemed to be a twin valley to that of the Ferrar Glacier, running parallel to it farther north. After a steep descent they found to their amazement that the glacier came to an abrupt halt. It was as though they had stepped through a magic door in Alice's Wonderland. Ahead of them lay a long valley completely free of snow and ice, carpeted with multi-colored boulders and lakes of many sizes. Here and there "hanging" glaciers seeped down over the clifflike valley walls, but never reached the foot. On all sides, 3,000 feet above them, ran a sharply defined line on the slopes which, Scott reported, clearly marked the level once reached by the glacial ice. It was thus apparent that at one time this part of Antarctica, at least, had been inundated with a much heavier blanket of ice.

By the time Scott returned to England the struggle to reach the North Pole was well underway and it was inevitable that men should start thinking about an effort to conquer its more inaccessible counterpart in the south. Shackleton had fully recovered from his siege of scurvy and in 1907 sought backing for an expedition which would try to reach both Antarctic poles—the Geographic Pole

Adélie penguins teem along the rocky shores of Wilkes Land.

A Weddell seal rears in anger at the sight of two-legged intruders. This fellow weighs about 800 pounds. ↓

← The Emperor penguin hatches its single egg in deep folds of abdominal flesh. This is the egg-exchanging ritual of the two parents.

Scott's party at the Pole. Hunger, snow-blindness, frost-bite, and heartbreak show in the faces of these men. The film of this picture was found with Scott's body.

Evidence of Antarctica's one-time verdancy is vividly imprinted in the rocks of that continent. This is a fossil fern.

at the bottom of the world and the Magnetic Pole which was believed to lie a few hundred miles inland from the coast of Victoria Land.

Using ponies to carry their supplies for the first leg of the trip, Shackleton and three companions set forth from Hut Point on November 3, 1908. After four weeks of slogging they passed the point achieved on the previous expedition and continued to follow the chain of mountains southward. It soon became evident that the range curved gradually to the east and that they would have to cross it to achieve the Pole. Within a few days they could see a gap in the mountains leading directly toward the Pole. They worked in toward its entrance and climbed a 3,000-foot mountain that would enable them to get a good view.

"From the top of this ridge," Shackleton wrote, "there burst upon our view an open road to the south, for there stretched before us a great glacier running almost south and north between two huge mountain ranges."

Never had men gazed on an ice river of such dimensions, for it averaged about fifteen miles in width and was 100 miles long. Shackleton named it Beardmore Glacier for one of his chief financial supporters.

It took them over two weeks to walk up the glacier. Once on top the four Britons set a direct course for the southernmost point on earth. They left one of the two remaining sledges with much of their food and warm clothes at the top of the glacier for the final 650-mile dash to the Pole and back. Constant winds from the south drove into their faces, blanching them with frostbite and slowing their progress. They had been marching hungry for two months, and it was beginning to show. They suffered from severe headaches and after every hour of pulling had to lie flat on their backs a few minutes. At last, on January 4, 1909, Shackleton realized they could not make it to the Pole and return alive.

Five days later, after being immobilized two days by a blizzard, they left their sledge behind and pressed another 18 miles south to within 112 miles of the Pole.

"We have shot our bolt," wrote Shackleton. "... While the Union Jack blew out stiffly in the icy gale that cuts us to the bone, we looked south with our powerful glasses, but could see nothing but the dead white snow plain. There was no break in the plateau as it extended towards the Pole, and we feel sure that the goal we have failed to reach lies on this plain. . . . Whatever regrets may be, we have done our best."

There followed a seven-week race with starvation. Their rations, reduced to compensate for delays, were barely enough to keep them alive, particularly since they were burning vast amounts of energy man-hauling their heavy sledges. Each blizzard which pinned them down threatened to drain their strength to the point where they could not make the next cache of food. "It is neck or nothing with us now," said Shackleton. "Our food lies ahead, and death stalks us from behind."

On January 25, a typical day, they had two meals, plus two stops for tea. The first meal consisted of two biscuits and two spoonfuls of cheese apiece. For the other they had hoosh—a pemmican stew—and one biscuit each. The next morning their food ran out altogether, and for two days they marched before reaching another cache. One of the party, Frank Wild, developed symptoms of dysentery and collapsed briefly one evening. The next day their breakfast consisted of one biscuit each. As he struggled weakly to prepare for the trail Wild found that Shackleton had shoved his own biscuit into his pocket. He insisted that Wild needed it more than he. "I do not suppose," wrote Wild in his diary, "that anyone else in the world can thoroughly realize how much generosity and sympathy was shown by this; *I do,* and *by God* I shall never forget it."

At length, nearing McMurdo Sound, they reached a well-stocked depot, and from then on they were safe.

While Shackleton was trying for the Geographic Pole —the point where all directions are north—three other members of his expedition made a trip to the vicinity of the South Magnetic Pole. T. W. Edgeworth David, professor of geology at Sydney University, led the group at the remarkable age of fifty-one. He was accompanied by Douglas Mawson, the expedition physicist, later to become Australia's foremost Antarctic explorer, and Dr. A. F. Mackay, a surgeon.

In somewhat incongruous fashion the great trek to the Magnetic Pole was begun by automobile—a four-cylinder "New Arrol-Johnston" with an engine that developed twelve to fifteen horsepower. The spoke-wheeled vehicle carried them only two miles, at which point the snowfall was so heavy that they decided to continue on foot. Towing the sledges themselves, they crossed McMurdo Sound and for 200 miles marched north over the

51

sea ice attached to the coast of Victoria Land. They then climbed Larsen Glacier to the inland plateau, across which they marched for almost three weeks.

On January 15 they set up their dip needle—a compass-type needle that shows the vertical, instead of the horizontal, direction of magnetic force. At the Magnetic Pole it points straight down. It was only 0.2° from the vertical, indicating that the vicinity of the Pole was about thirteen miles ahead of them. It was already known, by then, that the Magnetic Pole was an ephemeral point which wandered from hour to hour as well as from century to century. They left their instruments the next morning and hiked the additional thirteen miles. David wrote:

"...Mackay and I fixed up the flag-pole. We then bared our heads and hoisted the Union Jack at 3.30 p.m. with the words uttered by myself, in conformity with Lieutenant Shackleton's instructions, 'I hereby take possession of this area now containing the Magnetic Pole for the British Empire.' ... Then we gave three cheers for his Majesty the King."

They returned to the point on the coast where they had struck inland and were picked up by the *Nimrod,* which had returned to evacuate the expedition.

On March 4, 1909, the *Nimrod* set sail with all of Shackleton's expedition on board. The long trail south had been blazed. It remained for someone else to follow it the remaining 112 miles to the Pole.

6

The Pole

PROBABLY as long as the written word endures the tragic tale of Scott's march to the Pole will inspire the hearts of men. Within six months after the news of Shackleton's "near miss" reached London, Scott announced that he would try for the Pole himself. He intended to establish two bases, one in McMurdo Sound where he had placed his camp before and the other at the opposite end of the Ross Ice Shelf.

En route south, Scott received a cablegram from the Norwegian explorer Amundsen, who had been preparing an expedition to strike for the North Pole. The message read:

BEG LEAVE TO INFORM YOU PROCEEDING ANTARCTICA

There seemed little doubt that Amundsen intended to beat Scott to the Pole if he could. When the expedition ship *Terra Nova,* after depositing Scott at Cape Evans in McMurdo Sound, went to seek a base site at the eastern end of the Ross Ice Shelf, it found that Amundsen had established his base at the Bay of Whales, 450 miles to the east and 87 miles nearer the Pole.

Scott left Hut Point for his march to the Pole on November 3, 1911, three years to the day after Shackleton had set forth from the same spot. As with Shackleton, he used ponies for the first leg of the trek, but all the pulling had to be done by the men once they started up Beardmore Glacier. Scott took three four-man parties in contrast to Shackleton's single party of four. At the top of the glacier Scott sent one group back. The second party returned halfway from there to the Pole with the exception of Bowers, who was added to Scott's group.

A strange weakness had begun to affect them and Bowers, an exceptionally powerful man, was apparently added to the polar party to make up for this. No one knows for certain what was wrong, but it seems to have been scurvy or some other form of dietary deficiency. Their faithfully kept diaries reflect a suspicion that something was amiss, but they tended to lay the blame on head winds, intense cold, and soft snow that added to the burden of sledge hauling.

On January 16, as they moved south, Bowers suddenly saw a black speck ahead.

"We marched on," Scott wrote in his tent that night, "found that it was a black flag tied to a sledge bearer; near by the remains of a camp; sledge tracks and ski tracks going and coming and the clear trace of dogs' paws—many dogs. This told us the whole story. The Norwegians have forestalled us and are first at the Pole."

The next day, after they had reached their goal, Scott wrote:

"The Pole. Yes, but under very different circumstances from those expected. . . . Great God! this is an awful place and terrible enough for us to have laboured to it without the reward of priority.... Now for the run home and a desperate struggle. I wonder if we can do it."

Scott knew already that their situation was critical. It cannot be blamed on their shock at being beaten to the Pole by Amundsen, for the supporting party that left them two weeks earlier suffered the same symptoms.

From the start of their return journey the diaries of the Englishmen have an ominous tone. They seem to have known in their hearts that they could not make it. Even before leaving the Polar Plateau all were partially crippled in various ways. Wilson pulled a tendon in his leg; Oates' toes were black from prolonged frostbite; the hands of Edgar Evans were repeatedly frozen until the fingernails fell off. Scott fell and injured his shoulder.

Despite these danger signs, they lingered at the top of Beardmore Glacier to look for fossils which could tell the world what life existed on Antarctica in prehistoric times —and when. If they could "date a continent," it would be regarded by scientists as a far greater achievement than the Pole.

The next day they stopped again to collect specimens, but Scott noted in his diary, "Too tired to write geological notes." Three days later Scott said they were "in a very critical situation," yet Wilson dropped out of line again to go fossil hunting. After another four days of plodding down the glacier Evans' mind began to go. "A rather trying position," said Scott in his restrained fashion. "Evans has nearly broken down in brain, we think. He is absolutely changed from his normal, self-reliant self."

The next day, February 17, they were almost at the foot of the glacier, but Edgar Evans never made it. He kept dropping behind. At length, when the others were far ahead, they stopped for lunch to give him time to catch up, but the black speck in the distance drew no nearer. All four men skied back in alarm. "I was first to reach the poor man," said Scott, "and shocked at his appearance; he was on his knees with clothing disarranged, hands uncovered and frostbitten, and a wild look in his eyes. Asked what was the matter, he replied with a slow speech that he didn't know, but thought he must have fainted." They fetched the sledge and brought him to their camp, by which time he was in a coma. He died during the night. Wilson, who was a doctor, thought he must have been the victim of brain concussion.

There followed four weeks of constant suffering as they trudged north over the ice shelf. Their daily marches became steadily shorter and they complained that the snow had turned to sand under the sledge runners. Captain Oates of the Inniskilling Dragoons, with frozen feet and hands, was in the worst condition. At last one day, as they lay in their tent the canvas of which quivered in a blizzard, the air outside at about 40° below zero, Oates struggled to his lamed feet and said, "I am just going outside and may be some time." He never reappeared.

"We knew that poor Oates was walking to his death," said Scott, "but though we tried to dissuade him, we knew it was the act of a brave man and an English gentleman. We all hope to meet the end with a similar spirit, and assuredly the end is not far."

So weakened were they that their pace was half that of the outward march. Even on good days they could not make eight miles. At that speed their food would give out long before they could reach One-Ton Depot where ample supplies awaited them. They discarded their theodolite and camera to save weight but Wilson insisted that they must keep their bag of rock specimens on the sledge, to be "found with us or on our sledge."

On March 19, 1912, they camped within eleven miles of the big depot but were kept in their tent for days by a blizzard. This proved to be their last resting place. The day before they pitched their tent for the last time Scott had written, "The others are still confident of getting through—or pretend to be—I don't know!" Now they resigned themselves openly to death. As he lay slowly freezing, Scott composed twelve magnificent letters. In addition to a "Message to the Public," he wrote to Wilson's wife and Bowers' mother, to his own wife, and to some of his close friends, including Sir James Barrie, godfather to his son. "We are showing," he said to the playwright, "that Englishmen can still die with a bold spirit, fighting it out to the end." They were beyond hope, he told Barrie—feet frozen, food and fuel gone; "but it would do your heart good to be in our tent, to hear our songs and the cheery conversation as to what we will do when we get to Hut Point."

To his countrymen Scott felt obliged to explain the reasons for the disaster. He blamed it on a succession of misfortunes: the loss of nine ponies before the start of the polar trek, bad weather on the southbound trip, soft snow on the glacier, but above all the terrible cold and slow sledging surface which they encountered on their return march over the ice shelf. He wrote:

"Had we lived, I should have had a tale to tell of the hardihood, endurance, and courage of my companions which would have stirred the heart of every Englishman. These rough notes and our dead bodies must tell the tale, but surely, surely a great rich country like ours will see that those who are dependent on us are properly provided for."

After writing the letters, he made a final entry in his journal, dated March 29—ten days after they pitched their last camp:

". . . Every day we have been ready to start for our depot *11 miles* away, but outside the door of the tent it remains a whirling drift. I do not think we can hope for any better things now. We shall stick it out to the end, but we are getting weaker, of course, and the end cannot be far.

"It seems a pity, but I do not think I can write more.

R. Scott"

"Last entry," he wrote in an irregular hand:

"For God's sake look after our people."

The winter darkness came, snow sifted over the stiff forms in the tent. With spring a search party headed south to look for the expedition leader and his companions. Eleven miles beyond One-Ton Depot they passed what they thought was a snow cairn, but one man went closer and saw that it was a tent. The journals, letters, and two rolls of film were removed from under the bodies.

When developed the film produced some of the grimmest photographs ever taken—the men at the Pole, with heartbreak, suffering, snow-blindness, yet a will to carry on showing in each of their faces.

Near the tent the search party dug out the sledge, which they found to be laden with thirty-five pounds of rock specimens—a supercargo that must have felt like many hundred pounds to the dying men.

The other operations of Scott's last expedition have been overshadowed by the epic of the polar party, but they added greatly to the knowledge of Victoria Land from Cape Adare southward.

After World War II a moving picture was produced, entitled *Scott of the Antarctic*. No pains were spared to make it authentic, and once completed it was screened for some of the expedition survivors. For them the emotions aroused, as Frank Debenham, the geologist, put it, were almost insupportable.

"At times," he said, "especially towards the end of the film, some small thing like the pitiless sound of the blizzard or the ceaseless flapping of the tent would sweep away the intervening years and one was, once again, waiting at Cape Evans for Atkinson to bring the news from Hut Point and hearing, as he climbed up the ice-foot, 'The Pole Party has not returned,' and walking away in the semidarkness trying to take in that incredible sentence —'The Pole Party has not returned.' "

Amundsen's dash to the Pole was strikingly different from that of Scott in almost every respect. Scott was trained as a naval officer; the Norwegian was a professional explorer who had dreamed since boyhood of achieving the North Pole. His expedition was organized with that goal in mind, and only when he was forestalled by Peary did he pick the opposite point on the globe as second best. Norway was combed for ice pilots and men experienced both with skis and dog driving. The polar journey was to be entirely dependent on dogs—all the way to the Pole.

Amundsen placed his base at the Bay of Whales despite Shackleton's report that the floating shores of this indentation in the ice shelf were liable to break off unexpectedly and drift away. Amundsen correctly guessed that the bay was formed by land that divided the seaward flow of ice shelf, and placed his camp "Framheim" at the head of the bay where the ice appeared to be anchored by shoals. They had an advantage over the British in that their starting point was nearer the Pole. Nevertheless Scott was following a route already pioneered by Shackleton, while Amundsen and his four companions could only guess what obstacles lay in their path. The dogs proved a most reliable form of transport. During the four-week journey south over the ice shelf the men had to do little work. They either rode the sledges or coasted along on skis. They did not "race" for the Pole in that they spent two days at each of the main depots, resting the dogs and reorganizing the loads.

Three weeks out of Framheim they began to see great mountains ahead and to either side of their course. As they drew nearer, it became evident that this was the continuation of the mountain system which began in the vicinity of Cape Adare and ran at least 1,200 miles in a great arc embracing the Ross Sea and its extension under the Ross Ice Shelf. Scott, Shackleton, Amundsen, and all the others who have subsequently seen it have been struck by the massive, blocklike appearance of the mountains and by the horizontal layers of Beacon sandstone and other sedimentary rocks. This appears to be a great section of the earth's crust lifted in such a way that the layers have remained flat—what the geologists call a horst. Unlike other mountain systems such as the Andes, the Himalayas, and the Rockies, no name has yet been assigned to this system. Perhaps it can best be described as The Great Antarctic Horst.

The Norwegians did not find a broad ice river comparable to the Beardmore Glacier. After some probing they went up what they called the Axel Heiberg Glacier, which was comparatively narrow and steep, to an elevation of over 10,000 feet. Here they killed twenty-four of their weaker dogs. "It was hard—but it had to be so," wrote Amundsen. "We had agreed to shrink from nothing in order to reach our goal." The fact that both man and beast in Amundsen's party ate the dogs that weakened was one of their chief sources of strength.

On December 7 they passed Shackleton's farthest south camp, and the Norwegian flag was mounted to fly from one of the sledges for the rest of the trip to the Pole.

"No other moment of the whole trip affected me like this," Amundsen wrote. "The tears forced their way to my eyes; by no effort of will could I keep them back. It was the flag yonder that conquered me and my will. . . .

"We did not pass that spot without according our highest tribute of admiration to the man, who—together with his gallant companions—had planted his country's flag so infinitely nearer to the goal than any of his precursors. Sir Ernest Shackleton's name will always be written in the annals of Antarctic exploration in letters of fire."

A week later they were at the Pole. So efficient was their method of travel that, despite the need to pioneer a route up to the Polar Plateau, they made the journey in two weeks less time than their British competitors, arriving at the Pole a month ahead of them. In contrast to the British they felt sufficiently unhurried, with ample depots along their homeward route, to linger almost four days at the Pole, taking sun sights to make sure they were at the right spot. Before leaving, Amundsen, in case of possible disaster to his party, left in a tent at the Pole a letter to Scott enclosing a message to King Haakon VII of Norway. On the return trip the sun was so hot much of the time that it made them uncomfortable, and when they reached Framheim some of the dogs had actually gained weight.

The Norwegians boarded their ship *Fram* and headed for home, stopping off during March in Tasmania, where they basked in the first public acclaim of their achievement. Little did they or anyone else know that at that moment Scott, Wilson, and Bowers were slowly dying in a tent eleven miles from One-Ton Depot.

7

Great Things Done

WITH the Pole achieved, the second great challenge of Antarctica was the crossing of the continent. No one knew for sure whether the Antarctic was one or two land masses. There seemed to be two great breaks in its perimeter, one south of the Ross Sea on the Pacific side and the other south of the Weddell Sea. Some geographers thought that the two seas might join each other, splitting Antarctica in two.

In 1909 the German explorer and geophysicist Dr. Wilhelm Filchner proposed a march from the Weddell Sea across Antarctica to the Ross Sea. Although he was unable to achieve such a feat he was the first explorer to reach the south shore of the Weddell Sea. He found that coast to be a rampart of ice cliffs, much like that of the Ross Ice Shelf on the opposite side of Antarctica. Hardly had his men completed a barracks building when they heard a sound as though "hundreds of heavy guns had been fired at once." The ice shelf had broken up into bergs and they were drifting to sea. They managed to regain their ship, the *Deutschland,* only to become trapped in the ice pack, where they drifted for nine months before making their escape.

Several months after Filchner's return, Ernest Shackleton announced plans for an Imperial Trans-Antarctic Expedition that would march from Vahsel Bay on the Atlantic side to McMurdo Sound on the Pacific. A party based at McMurdo would lay depots of food along the route between there and the Beardmore Glacier.

To venture into the treacherous Weddell Sea, Shackleton obtained a stout new Norwegian vessel, which he named the *Endurance*. Mawson's ship *Aurora* was procured to carry the McMurdo Sound party.

Shackleton in the *Endurance* followed the shore almost to the stretch discovered by Filchner, but before he could reach Vahsel Bay he was forced out of sight of land by pack ice which on January 19, 1915, closed around the ship so tightly that she could not move. As subsequent weeks passed it was apparent that she was beset.

At first the ship appeared to be safe, for it was frozen into a platter of ice three miles long and two and a half miles wide. This was an effective buffer against assaults by other floes. Gradually there was more and more evidence of compression in the pack and by July the floes on all sides had begun to buckle into pressure ridges. On August 1 the floe cracked right through the position of the ship, exposing her hull to the same twisting motion that had broken the ice.

For several months the *Endurance* withstood the pressure but finally she began to take water, and on October 27 they had to abandon the ship. "It was a sickening sensation to feel the decks breaking up under one's feet, the great beams bending and then snapping with a noise like heavy gunfire," Shackleton wrote. "The floes, with the

64

Photo by Frank Hurley

Crushed by the pack, the Endurance *is kept from sinking only by the grip of the ice. One of Shackleton's dogteams takes a last look.*

The mighty Snow Cruiser begins its descent from the deck of the North Star at Little America.

Admiral Byrd at his radio in the hut where he almost died of carbon monoxide poisoning.

force of millions of tons of moving ice behind them, were simply annihilating the ship."

The nearest food and shelter was at Paulet Island, 346 miles away across the drifting pack. There stood the hut built by the Swedes in 1902, which was stocked with supplies purchased by Shackleton himself for the relief of that expedition. He intended to lead the party in that direction, with men and dogs dragging sledges laden not only with food and camping gear but also with their boats. Not an ounce of weight could be carried that did not contribute to their chances of survival. Symbolically Shackleton took out his precious gold watch, a gold cigarette case, and all his gold sovereigns, and threw them away. The others followed suit.

The epic of endurance, ingenuity, and perseverance that followed is probably the most remarkable in Antarctic history. For five months they remained on the drifting ice floes, living on seals and penguins, waiting for the pack to open up so that they could launch their boats. There was constant danger of the floes' cracking under them. When they did so, Shackleton's men would suddenly have to shift themselves and their supplies to a more solid piece of ice.

In April the pack opened up. They launched their boats, piled everything aboard, and began threading their way toward land. Soon they found themselves contending with stormy seas. Worse still, they had not stocked up on water while in the pack and found themselves rowing with parched mouths, hauling on ice-encrusted oars.

On April 15, after many hardships, they reached Ele-

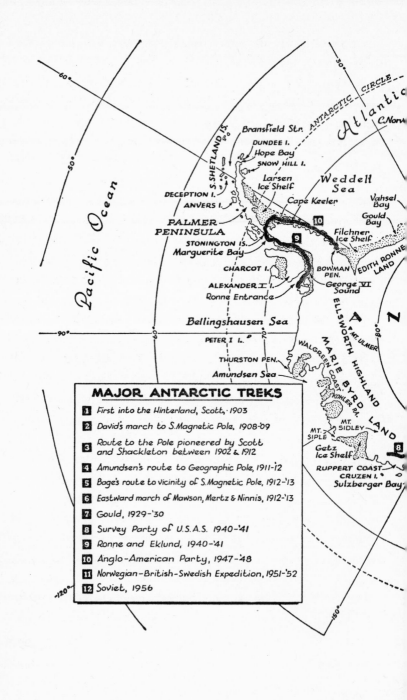

MAJOR ANTARCTIC TREKS

1. First into the Hinterland, Scott, 1903
2. David's march to S. Magnetic Pole, 1908-09
3. Route to the Pole pioneered by Scott and Shackleton between 1902 & 1912
4. Amundsen's route to Geographic Pole, 1911-12
5. Bage's route to vicinity of S. Magnetic Pole, 1912-'13
6. Eastward march of Mawson, Mertz & Ninnis, 1912-'13
7. Gould, 1929-'30
8. Survey Party of U.S.A.S. 1940-'41
9. Ronne and Eklund, 1940-'41
10. Anglo-American Party, 1947-'48
11. Norwegian-British-Swedish Expedition, 1951-'52
12. Soviet, 1956

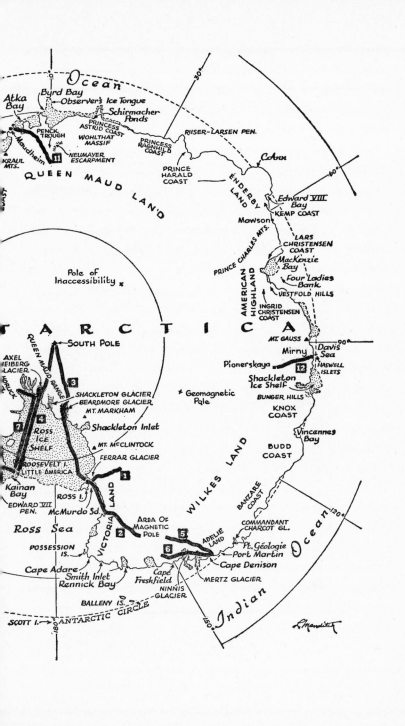

phant Island, a mountainous, largely ice-covered fragment of land north of Palmer Peninsula. One man's feet had become so badly frozen in the boat that five of his toes had to be amputated. The operation was done in their makeshift hut ashore with only a blubber stove to take the chill off and provide boiling water for sterilization. Fortunately two surgeons, Drs. McIlroy and Macklin, were in the party. Other men were becoming demoralized by their prolonged hardships. It was over a year since they had become beset in the ice. Only the forceful leadership of Shackleton and Wild forestalled trouble.

From Elephant Island Shackleton and five picked men set forth on one of the most remarkable small-boat voyages in history. Their aim was to sail to South Georgia, 870 miles away, and get help for the twenty-two men left behind. The seas which had to be crossed are generally regarded as the stormiest in the world, and they did not temper their anger for the little craft, only 22½ feet long with a 6-foot beam. For two weeks they fought a succession of gales. The boat pitched wildly, but stayed upright, even though half filled with water. They bailed almost constantly to keep from foundering.

On May 8 they saw the black cliffs and icy summits of South Georgia. The next morning at daybreak they landed in a little cove on King Haakon Bay and found a cave where they fell into exhausted sleep in their wet clothes. The next day they gathered dry tussock grass to spread on the floor of the cave and hung the boat's sails over its entrance. A wood fire helped to dry their clothes.

Shackleton and two other members of the party then set out for Husvik on the east coast of South Georgia, leaving the other three members behind. In a letter of instructions to Harry McNeish, a Scottish carpenter with the expedition whom he left in charge, he said: "You will remain here until relief arrives. You have ample seal food which you can supplement with birds and fish according to your skill. You are left with a double barrelled gun, 50 cartridges [other supplies listed]. . . . You also have all the necessary equipment to support life for an indefinite period in the event of my non-return. You had better after winter is over try and sail round to the East Coast. The course I am making towards Husvik is *East* magnetic. I trust to have you relieved in a few days."

Although there had been whaling stations for many years on the coast that lay twenty miles to the east, no one had ever penetrated into the island's ice-capped interior. It is doubtful that Shackleton and his two companions could have crossed the glaciers and descended the perilous ice falls in their weakened condition but for Shackleton's fund of experience in such work. In less than two days they were descending the slopes toward the whaling station, whose whistle, calling the men to work, came to them faintly through the chilly air.

The first people they met backed away in alarm, until they learned that the shaggy emaciated figure before them was Sir Ernest Shackleton. A whaler was immediately sent to fetch McNeish and the others on the opposite side of the island. The rescue of the main party on Elephant

Island was not so easy. Five successive relief expeditions were organized, until the steamer *Yelcho* succeeded in breaking through. The men on Elephant Island had been there almost twenty weeks when rescued.

It is probably fair to say that Shackleton's achievement in leading his expedition to safety without losing a single man—despite almost unbelievable hazards—was a far greater claim to enduring fame than if he had fulfilled his goal of crossing the continent.

While the men of the *Endurance* were fighting for survival in the Weddell Sea, the other part of the Shackleton expedition was struggling to lay depots for a transcontinental party that was never to come. Ten men were put ashore at Cape Evans on McMurdo Sound and their ship, the *Aurora*, tied up nearby to be frozen in for the winter. During a storm on May 7, the men looked out of their hut and saw to their horror that the ice and their ship, bearing a large portion of their food and equipment, were gone.

When spring came they set out with the meager supplies that were left to lay the depots on which the lives of the Transcontinental Party would be dependent. On the return trip scurvy struck the four members of the depot-laying party, and one man, the Reverend A. P. Spencer-Smith, died after being dragged for forty days on a sledge. Two others were blown out to sea during a blizzard as the ice broke up while they were trying to cross the sound to their camp at Cape Evans. The supreme irony lay in the fact that they had fought against almost hopeless odds to fulfill their obligations in a scheme that had already failed. Had they been in radio contact with Shackleton, the long months of suffering and the lives of three men would have been spared, but the early radio models with which they had been supplied were ineffective.

The *Aurora,* after drifting for nine months in the pack, broke out and was able to reach New Zealand for repairs. There Shackleton joined her to help in the relief operation, and on January 10, 1917, she sailed into McMurdo Sound where the survivors of the depot-laying operations had been forced to spend another winter.

Before embarking, they erected a cross in memory of their three lost comrades and penned an epitaph which they placed in a copper cartridge at the foot of the cross. There it was found thirty years later by an American expedition. Written from memory, primarily from Browning's "Prospice," it read:

> Things done for gain are nought
> But great things done endure.
>
> —I ever was a fighter so one fight more
> The best and the last
> I should hate that death bandaged
>   my eyes and bid me creep past.
>
> Let me pay in a minute Life's glad
>   arrears of pain, darkness & cold.

71

It seemed a fitting epitaph, as well, for the "Heroic Era" of Antarctic exploration which had drawn to an end. From now on modern techniques of communications and travel would not eliminate the dangers of penetrating the unknown, but never again would explorers cast off all ties with the outside world when they ventured into the polar regions.

8

The First Flights

I T WAS NOT until a decade after Shackleton's return that the attention of the world again turned to Antarctica. By then a new instrument of exploration had appeared—the airplane. Three men were to bring the Air Age to the Antarctic: Byrd, Wilkins, and Ellsworth.

Wilkins made the first airplane flight in that region, while Ellsworth accomplished the remarkable feat of crossing the continent in a single-engine plane. But it was the name of Richard Evelyn Byrd which was to dominate the history of Antarctica for the next three decades.

Born in 1888 of a distinguished Virginia family, Byrd was trained as a naval aviator during World War I and became interested in pioneer long-range flights. His initial polar experience was as commander of the naval aviation unit assigned to the MacMillan Arctic Expedition which explored Greenland in 1925. He achieved national fame in 1926 when he and another naval aviator, Floyd Bennett, flew over the North Pole.

At the time of his death in 1957 Byrd had played a leading role in the dispatch of five expeditions to the Antarctic, the last being *Operation Deepfreeze*, scheduled to remain there until 1959. For his early expeditions very little support was available from the government, and he had to organize and promote them as a private individual. Two men, in particular, helped make it possible for him to take off on his epoch-making flights. They were John D. Rockefeller, Jr., and Edsel Ford.

Sailing south in 1928 for his first Antarctic expedition with two ships, the *City of New York* and *Eleanor Bolling*, Byrd selected the Bay of Whales as his base. Upon his arrival he built the most elaborate community yet constructed in Antarctica. There were three main structures, plus more than a dozen smaller huts and aircraft hangars. The forty-two inhabitants of what came to be known as Little America were by far the largest party ever to winter in Antarctica.

When Byrd sailed south he brought with him the American technique of doing things in a "big way." A total of 665 tons of cargo was unloaded and moved by dogteam to the camp site. The crates of supplies were stacked in parallel walls in such a manner that, when roofed over and buried in the fast-drifting snow, they helped provide tunnels linking all the principal buildings. Electric lights and even telephones were installed.

The expedition had three ski-equipped monoplanes: a big tri-motored Ford in which Byrd planned to fly over the Pole, a Fokker, and a Fairchild. On January 27, 1929, Byrd made his first important exploratory flight in Antarctica. He and his companions set their course for Scott's Nunataks, the only charted landmark to the eastward, whose known position would be a good point from which to strike into the unknown. To provide for a forced landing the little plane was loaded down with equipment and trail rations comparable to those carried on the long sledging journeys of an earlier generation.

They followed the edge of the ice shelf to what was then known as Edward VII "Land," sighting several small peaks far inland. Past Scott's Nunataks snow squalls forced them to turn back just as they caught sight of what appeared to be frozen-over ocean on the far side of Edward VII "Land"—the first clue that it was in fact a peninsula.

They then headed south for the peaks seen on the outward flight. These proved to be fourteen summits, scattered in a broad crescent. This range, his first important discovery, Byrd named the Rockefeller Mountains.

"The great ice sheet had folded over them," he wrote, "burying all but the highest peaks and filling the valleys to overflowing. It was a scene of extraordinary beauty and simplicity. One could not resist the impression that the peaks were struggling to lift their heads above the eternal snows."

With this flight, Byrd felt that the effectiveness of the airplane as an instrument of exploration had been demonstrated. At times they discovered new lands at the rate of 4,000 square miles an hour, Byrd said, recording on their aerial cameras unmapped coasts and mountains whose exploration by dogteam would have taken many months.

Before the advent of the winter night Laurence Gould, geologist and second in command of the expedition, was anxious to wield his hammer on the newly discovered Rockefeller Mountains 130 miles to the east. On March

7 he landed with a small party on a frozen melt-water lake at the southern end of the Rockefellers. For a week Gould reported each day by radio that all was well, but then his transmissions suddenly stopped. A search plane, sent out with Byrd aboard, at length spotted a column of smoke and a flash of light from Gould's camp. About three-quarters of a mile away was the wreck of the Fokker.

When Byrd landed he was told of the freak accident. Periodic gales of almost incredible intensity had beset the party. The plane was secured to lines fastened to moorings frozen into the ice, but in the constant gales its skis rose four or five inches off the snow. While they were in their tent a gust more intense than the others—Gould thought it was about 150 miles an hour—tore the plane from its moorings and it rose into backward flight, its propeller spinning as though the engine were running, and crashed in the distance.

As the Fairchild had been loaded to capacity on its rescue flight, Byrd and Hanson, the radio operator, had to remain with Gould while the rest of Gould's party rode back to Little America. It was three days before the plane could return for the others. Meanwhile Byrd "ran" his expedition from the little tent in the Rockefeller Mountains. He was over 100 miles from his base or the nearest depot—more isolated than Scott had been when he lay freezing in his tent seventeen years earlier—but what a change had taken place in exploration! Through his trail radio Byrd was in touch with Little America, with dogteams on the trail, with his ships in New Zealand; he even transacted business with his office in New York.

During the winter night, Byrd and his men made extensive preparations for the coming season. The central objective was the flight to the Pole, but also of great importance was the geological journey to be led by Larry Gould. This, it was hoped, could examine not only the Queen Maud Range that straddled the route to the Pole, but also the mountains reported by Amundsen to lie east of the Ross Ice Shelf.

On November 25 Byrd took off, with the veteran Norwegian pilot Bernt Balchen at the controls, for the flight to the bottom of the world. The plane had been loaded with the maximum amount of fuel, survival rations, and equipment which the engines were capable of lifting to an elevation of 11,000 feet.

Byrd thought of the difference between this journey to the Pole and that of Amundsen. "We had the advantages of swiftness and comfort," he said, "but we had as well an enlarged fallibility. A flaw in a piece of steel, a bit of dirt in the fuel lines or carburetor jets, a few hours of strong head winds, fog or storm—these things, remotely beyond our control, could destroy our carefully laid plans. . . . "

Byrd chose Liv Glacier, to the right of Heiberg, as it seemed broader and lower. They flew into the giant chasm down which this ice river cascaded from the Polar Plateau to the floating shelf. Ahead of them ice falls and terraces rose higher than the elevation of the plane. The engines were pulling smoothly. Could they lift the load high enough? Ten miles up the glacier—about a quarter of the way to the top—its surface was cracked open into a procession of terrible crevasses. The air, too, roughened, for a river of cold air was racing down off the plateau through the chasm. The force of this wind became more and more intense, until they realized that it was damping their climb. The altimeters read 9,600 feet, and there were indications that the plane was close to its ceiling with its present load. The pass ahead narrowed so that there could be no turning back.

"Balchen began to yell and gesticulate," Byrd wrote, ". . . the meaning was manifest. 'Overboard—overboard —200 pounds!'"

Out the door went one bag of food, but the downdraft became even more severe and the plane's line of flight was still below the top of the pass. "More," Balchen shouted. "Another bag." They pushed it through the trapdoor and saw it burst on the surface of the glacier, scattering the provisions. The plane gained new buoyancy and cleared the pass by 500 feet. They crept through at less than ninety miles an hour, but the battle was won.

Amundsen and Scott had been unable to see anything in the region beyond the Pole except the endless plateau. It was the same with Byrd, roughly 1,500 feet above the surface. At the Pole they dropped an American flag weighted with a stone from the grave of Floyd Bennett, Byrd's companion on the North Pole flight, who had died in the interim. They returned to Little America without difficulty, less than nineteen hours after their departure.

A week later, on December 5, Byrd flew east on what, geographically, was a more important flight than that to the Pole. It reached beyond the 150th meridian into a region larger than Alaska which, as Byrd put it, was unseen, unknown, and unclaimed.

In the interests of reliable navigation Byrd again flew past Scott's Nunataks and out over the ice-strewn sea which lay beyond. He wrote:

"We could now see into the great blank space on the chart which I had studied hundreds of times and wondered about.

"About 12:40 o'clock the thing we were looking for emerged grudgingly from the translucent horizon—first a mountainous mass a few degrees to the right of our course. . . . As we drew nearer other peaks loomed up, and there was the suggestion of a long range. It was, we knew, a first class discovery."

The mountains, arrayed in a succession of ranges, ran north and south for a distance of 180 miles on the far side of a vast bay. Having christened the Rockefeller Mountains for one of the expedition's chief sponsors, he named these new mountains for Edsel Ford.

Meanwhile, the Geological Party under Gould had reached the Queen Maud Mountains and begun its surveying and geological work. The foothills, Gould found, were pre-Cambrian—the oldest of rocks—but the higher mountains, such as Fridtjof Nansen, were capped with level layers of sandstone. The sandstone cliffs were interlaid with seams of low-grade coaly material.

They worked eastward along the foot of the mountains, discovering a number of great glaciers that emptied into the Ross Ice Shelf to the east of those sighted by Amundsen. After skirting the façade of the range for 125 miles they found themselves well past Longitude 150° West. This meant that they were in the hitherto unclaimed and unsighted sector which Byrd had decided to name for his wife.

Gould and his companions climbed a small peak which they named Supporting Party Mountain, in tribute to the men who had placed the depots that made their trek possible. In a cairn on the summit they placed a note which said in part:

"We are beyond or east of the 150th meridian, and therefore in the name of Commander Richard Evelyn Byrd claim this land as a part of Marie Byrd Land, a dependency or possession of the United States of America."

They then set their course for Little America, arriving there on January 19, 1930, after eleven weeks and 1,500 miles on the trail.

Byrd returned to a hero's welcome in the United States. A joint resolution of Congress extended the gratitude of the nation for his achievements; he was made a rear admiral on the retired list; and when his ship arrived at the Washington Navy Yard, President Hoover himself came to greet the expedition—an unprecedented honor.

9

Byrd Returns to Antarctica

HAVING OPENED the door to Marie Byrd Land, the great region east of Little America, Byrd wished to step through it and in 1933 he again headed south, with a small wooden ice ship, the *Bear,* and a cargo ship, the *Jacob Ruppert.*

Edsel Ford was again one of his chief backers, and the names of others are preserved on the map of Antarctica: Watson Escarpment, named for the head of the International Business Machines Corporation; the Horlick Mountains, named for the malted milk manufacturer; the Walgreen Coast, named for the drugstore operator; and the Ruppert Coast, named for the New York brewer.

As a pioneer in aviation Byrd sought on each of his expeditions to develop new polar transport techniques. On his first trip to Antarctica he brought a "snowmobile" —a Ford chassis with skis in front and caterpillar treads in place of rear wheels. It hauled a load seventy-five miles south of Little America, but then broke down. This time Byrd obtained a massive six-ton tractor, known as the Cletrac, and three vehicles made by André Citroën, the French car maker, which were, in effect, light trucks mounted on tracks much like snowmobiles.

The expedition also brought four aircraft, including

a Kellett autogyro—uncle of the modern helicopter. The largest plane was a Curtiss-Wright Condor, a biplane that could take off on skis or on floats.

The camp at Little America was found intact, although sagging under its five-year load of snow. Eight new buildings were erected on top of the old ones, with connecting passages between the two camps.

Before leaving Boston Byrd had secretly prepared a scheme for wintering far south in the interior of Antarctica. A special boxlike cabin had been constructed for use in this project. The purpose of the "Advance Base" would be to study weather near the South Pole during the period of continuous darkness. It was obvious that the torrents of cold air which pour off the Polar Plateau must have a profound influence on the earth's weather, but nothing was known of inland meteorology during the Antarctic winter.

On March 16, 1934, the three Citroëns and the Cletrac headed south hauling the supplies and prefabricated hut for Advance Base. It was a procession of vehicles such as never had been seen in Antarctica—thirteen tons of mechanized equipment in one caravan.

Sixty-seven miles out the Cletrac broke down and this halved the hauling capacity of the convoy. It meant that Advance Base would have to be set up at "100-Mile Depot," 123 statute miles south of Little America. To protect the hut against wind and the more extreme periods of cold, it was set in a pit dug in the ice shelf, the roof flush with the surface. A trapdoor in the roof gave access to the open air, and the supplies were stored in tunnels that led off from a vestibule alongside the hut.

The question arose as to who should man the station. The breakdown in transport meant, Byrd said, that the supplies were insufficient for three men; yet he was reluctant to station two there.

"Life in that spot," he wrote, "would resemble life on a dark, dead, and bitterly cold planet, and for some months would be almost as inaccessible as on that planet.

"Two men, jammed together at arm's length in a tiny shack in this strange environment, living by the dim light of a lantern in a state of perpetual congestion and intrusion, staring at each other for seven months; hardly able to take a step without coming into collision; unable to express a thought without running athwart the other man's prejudices; small things taking on a monstrous significance! What man's nerves could stand the irritation?"

Hence Byrd resolved to stand the long vigil by himself.

On March 28 all was ready. The tractor men headed their machines back for Little America and Byrd watched them disappear like black bugs over the white prairie, clouds of white smoke rising from their exhausts in the cold air.

Byrd, as he described later in his book *Alone,* fell into a daily routine of weather observations, improving his little camp, hauling in the electric generator to heat it on the stove, so that it could be started for each scheduled radio contact with Little America. He was provided with a well-stocked library and, so long as gales did not make it hazardous, he took walks around the sunken camp. Above the surface the only evidence of his station was a cluster of weather instruments. For communications the main base transmitted voice broadcasts and Byrd replied with a keyed signal. The latter was impersonal and for a long time concealed the true state of affairs at Advance Base. Byrd, not being a professional operator, transmitted only about ten words a minute, and when it became even slower not much notice was taken at first.

About six weeks after the start of his isolation, Byrd noticed that something was wrong. He could not concentrate as he tried to read in the evening. The words ran together on the page, his eyes hurt, and he had a mild headache. "I've been strangely irritable all day, and since supper have been depressed," he wrote in his diary. ". . . I can't find any single thing to account for the mood. Yet, it has been there; and tonight, for the first time, I must admit the problem of keeping my mind on an even keel is a serious one."

He reviewed the possible causes and finally his suspicions focused on the stove. It was a caboose-style coal stove rigged with a single oil burner. There were cracks in the joints of the stove pipe and he found that the ventilators which supplied fresh air to the hut were repeatedly clogged with ice and snow. He cleared the vents and closed the cracks as best he could, and soon felt better.

On May 31, after he had spent almost an hour and a half exchanging radio messages with various members of his staff at Little America, the gasoline generator which powered his radio began missing. He signaled "wait" and went into the snow tunnel where the engine was running. There was something wrong, for the tunnel was full of exhaust gases. After adjusting the needle valve, he straightened up and apparently filled his lungs with carbon monoxide gas, for he regained consciousness on his knees. Here, near the snow floor of the tunnel, the air was breathable. With a supreme effort he returned to the radio and signed off.

"My actions thereafter are uncertain," he wrote. "I don't really know which were nightmare and which were fact. I remember lying on the bunk, fully dressed, and hearing, as if with surprise, the irregular beat of the engine in the tunnel and realizing that I must shut it off to escape asphyxiation. Dizziness seized me, and my heart turned fantastic somersaults. . . ."

Staggering like a drunken man, crawling part of the way, he reached the tunnel and threw the ignition switch.

He did not recover from this carbon monoxide poisoning throughout the winter. For a long time he was unable to keep food in his stomach, and there seemed little chance that he could survive the winter night. As he was farther south than any man had ever wintered, the period of total darkness lasted four months. As long as he could stand he struggled up the ladder to keep up his weather records, but his last reserves of energy he saved for the radio contacts with Little America three times a week. He feared that, if he let slip a clue as to his true condition, a rescue attempt would be made, in the winter night, which might cost the lives of several more men. For a long time his deception was successful.

In July the temperature dropped to 80° below zero. The air, when he went up onto the surface, caused his throat to clamp shut so that he could not breathe unless he faced downwind and sheltered his face. He tried to use the stove as little as possible; he ate half-frozen food; but he could not allow himself to freeze to death. "This fire was my enemy," he said, "but I could not live without it."

Poulter, his second-in-command, wanted to visit Advance Base before the close of the winter night to observe meteors simultantaneously with Little America in an effort to determine their height. He asked Byrd's approval of such a venture. To Byrd this meant a chance of survival. He told Poulter to come if he thought he could make the trip safely, but added that he must return to Little America immediately if he could not follow the trail flags. These had been set along the route at intervals of one-sixth of a mile and, presumably, so long as a vehicle kept to the trail in the darkness, it would be safe from crevasses.

On July 20 Poulter set forth, but lost the trail and was forced to turn back. At Little America the suspicion had at last taken root that something was wrong with the expedition leader. His ragged transmissions and the frequency with which he signaled "wait," followed by long pauses, indicated more than just the "bad arm" which was his explanation. After twice again being turned back by engine trouble, Poulter set out once more on August 8 with two companions. Luck was with them this time.

They picked up the old trail and in two days were within twenty miles of Advance Base.

Byrd feared that in the darkness the tractor would pass close by his camp and never see it. He constantly fired flares into the sky and flew kites with flaming tails. On August 10, as he emerged from his trapdoor and automatically looked to the northern horizon, he saw a beam of light lift from the Barrier, sweep up to the stars, down and up again; then vanish.

Stumbling in his excitement, he hitched a flare to a kite and a blindingly bright light rose into the air. Several hours later the appearances of the light to the north were more frequent and at last he could see another light, fixed and dim—a headlight. Finally the rattle of the machine reached his ears, and the "beep-beep-beep" of its little French horn.

His first words were said to have been, "Come on down, fellows. I have a bowl of hot soup for you."

Although they had been sure that something was amiss, they were not prepared for the man who greeted them:

". . . we were shocked at his appearance," Poulter wrote. "Emaciated, hollow-cheeked, weak, and haggard though he was, he met us casually, calmer by far than any of us . . . but his ghastly condition and husky voice told us that, in spite of this matter-of-factness he had been through some terrific things."

The three men moved in with Byrd and helped nurse him back to health until, two months later, a plane from Little America flew him back to his headquarters.

In September and October the trail parties took to the field. Their mobility was greatly aided by the Citroën tractors, on which cabins had been constructed containing bunks, stoves, and radios. One Citroën headed east to establish food and fuel depots for a group led by Paul Siple, who as a Boy Scout had accompanied Byrd on his first trip to Little America. The vehicle passed south of the Rockefeller Mountains and reached Mount Grace McKinley in the Edsel Ford Ranges. Within three weeks it was back in Little America, its mission accomplished after covering 525 miles. Mechanized surface travel in Antarctica had come into its own.

Two parties headed south along the trail past Advance Base. One, led by Quin Blackburn, was to extend the work of the first Byrd expedition eastward from Supporting Party Mountain. To reach the Polar Plateau it ascended an ice river, now known as Scott Glacier. It took the members of this party ten days to reach the summit, where they found a peak—Mount Weaver—rising naked from the plateau. In its rocky walls, only 210 miles from the Pole, were a dozen clearly defined seams of coal, and in nearby moraines they found a profusion of fossils, including numerous fragments of tree trunks from a foot to eighteen inches thick. On the glacier they collected lichens, growing primarily on the north faces where they were sheltered from the wind and favored by the sun.

These are still the southernmost finds of plant life, both prehistoric and contemporary. The record is likely to stand for a long time, as there appears to be little or no exposed land south of Mount Weaver. Low-grade coal had now been discovered in every sector of the Great Antarctic Horst examined by geologists—further evidence that immense coal fields cap the entire polar area.

After five days on the plateau, they started back for Little America. They were on the trail almost three months and covered 1,410 miles—farther than the longest flight made by the expedition.

Another group sought, by seismic soundings, to determine the thickness of the ice sheet. The technique was essentially that used in oil prospecting, where an explosion is set off and echoes from the buried rock layers are recorded. In this case the interval before an echo was heard off the rock bed under the ice sheet would indicate its thickness.

The members of the seismic party set off their charges at ten points on the Marie Byrd Land plateau and, after their 815-mile journey, reported that when they were camped at from 2,000 to 3,000 feet above sea level the ice beneath them was roughly 1,000 to 2,000 feet thick.

The Eastern Party of four men under Siple reached far into the virgin territory of Marie Byrd Land. They achieved the northern part of the Edsel Ford Mountains and brought back a wealth of geological and biological specimens. The sterile landscape of the Edsel Ford Mountains proved to be far from barren of life. In addition to a couple of dozen varieties of moss and lichen, Siple brought back small vials of stained ice which he had chipped from pools of melt-water in the mountains, from patches of slime near a receding glacier, and such spots. When melted and placed under a microscope these fragments came astir with a bustling to and fro of countless microscopic creatures—rotifers, water bears, and various types of infusoria.

The second Byrd expedition, in many hitherto untried ways, had sought to probe the scientific mysteries of Antarctica. Its large scientific staff had not only delved into the traditional sciences of the explorer—geology and biology—but had extended cosmic ray research and fixed weather observations into the highest southern latitudes yet achieved and had for the first time sought, by seismic survey, to determine the thickness of the ice sheet capping the bottom of the globe.

10

Across the Continent

PROBABLY the most courageous flight ever made in the Antarctic was that of Lincoln Ellsworth across the continent. For years this feat had beckoned adventurous fliers. The idea was born with the attempt of an Australian, Sir Hubert Wilkins, to fly from the Weddell Sea to the Ross Sea, following the coastline. Although his was the first flight made in Antarctic regions, he never completed the long hop he had planned.

Ellsworth was first gripped by the lure of Antarctica in 1913 while standing in St. Paul's Cathedral in London during a memorial service to Robert Falcon Scott. In 1925 he and Amundsen attempted unsuccessfully to reach the North Pole in two seaplanes.

Ten years later, after two frustrated efforts in previous seasons, he set forth to fly across Antarctica, starting from Dundee Island off the northeast tip of Palmer Peninsula. Wilkins accompanied him on his ship, the *Wyatt Earp*, named after the frontier marshal of Dodge City and Tombstone, for whom he had a passionate admiration, and his pilot was Herbert Hollick-Kenyon.

Ellsworth's plan was a daring one. He had brought no weather man on his expedition, feeling, as he put it, "that it is impossible to forecast in the Antarctic." Instead he proposed to land on the ice sheet whenever he encountered poor conditions and wait for the sky to clear. He had carefully studied the reports of those who had traveled the Antarctic trail and felt that rarely were the sastrugi—wind-blown ridges in the snow surface—sufficiently high to trip a plane that was landing on skis. As long as he set down before entering an area of poor visibility, he felt he could find a safe spot. Once on the surface, the chief danger was that the plane would blow away in a gale, as had happened to Byrd's Fokker. To avoid this he chose a low-winged monoplane specially made for him by the Northrop Airplane Company. By digging trenches for the skis Ellsworth hoped he could lower the plane until its wings were flush with the snow, so the wind could not get under them.

Probably no man has ever flown with such boldness into the unknown, for the country which he intended to cross in a single-engined plane was a blank on the maps almost the entire way. Once he had passed the midpoint there was no turning back.

He and Hollick-Kenyon flew down the Palmer Peninsula until a great wall of mountains appeared ahead of them. "Bold and rugged peaks, bare of snow, rose almost sheer to some 12,000 feet above sea level," Ellsworth wrote. "Impressed with the thought of eternity and our insignificance, I named the new mountains the Eternity Range." They flew on at an altitude of 10,000 feet until, three hours later, the mountains had vanished in favor of a vast inland ice plateau. For the first 1,000 miles they had maintained radio contact with the ship, but now their transmitter failed. They were almost halfway, since Little America was 1,300 miles ahead of them, and decided to continue on.

Rising through the white crust over the continent an isolated mountain group appeared, surmounted by a peak about 13,000 feet high, which Ellsworth named Mount Mary Louise Ulmer for his wife. Soon thereafter they sighted another range about 100 miles to the south, and due to increasing haze they decided to land.

They had been in the air almost fourteen hours on this first leg of the flight. "We climbed out of the plane rather stiffly and stood looking around in the heart of the Antarctic," said Ellsworth. "There we were—two lone human beings in the midst of an ice-capped continent two-thirds the size of North America."

He raised the American flag in this lonely spot and claimed the land between 80° and 120° West for the United States, "so far as the act would allow." This embraced the territory lying between the British claim and Marie Byrd Land, which already had been declared American territory by Admiral Byrd.

After nineteen hours they took off, but within a half hour were forced to land again by thick-looking weather ahead. Three days later they made another short hop, and then for eight days they lay in their tent or worked to ready the plane for flight, only to be driven back to their shelter by another blizzard. The howling gale packed snow into the plane, filling even the tail, and Ellsworth, the thinner of the pair, spent an entire day with a teacup, carefully scooping the snow from around the controls. Desperate at the long delay, they decided to take off even if the weather were not promising.

They unloaded the plane and roared the engine to lift it out of the trenches in which it had been moored. This time luck was with them. The western horizon became clear and they flew to within 150 miles of the Bay of Whales before landing to determine their position. They found themselves close to sea level on the edge of the Ross Ice Shelf. The next morning, December 5, they flew within twenty miles of Little America but did not realize they were off course. "From the air we saw the ice-free waters of Ross Sea, the goal of my four years of endeavor," Ellsworth wrote, but fifteen minutes later the engine spluttered. Their fuel was exhausted and they had to land. This was their fifth camp on the transcontinental journey. For three days snow and wind kept them in camp, and then they began a heartbreaking effort to find Byrd's abandoned base. On the ninth, thinking they saw on the horizon the snow-covered buildings and the wind generator atop one of the radio towers, they loaded ten days' food on a sledge and set off, leaving behind their tent and sextant.

It could have been a fatal error. After tramping nine miles, they found that they had been deluded by pinnacles and humps of pressure ice. Fortunately, they were able to find their way back to the plane. A round of sun sights showed them to be twelve miles south of the Bay of Whales, and they set forth again, this time fully equipped. By the time they found the base, they had been on the ice shelf ten days. Breaking a skylight, they slipped into the welcome shelter of Little America and were picked up by ship a month later.

Ellsworth's transcontinental flight has been likened by geographers to the venture of Nansen who, on the basis of his studies, believed that he could safely allow his ship to become frozen into the Arctic pack and would thus be carried near the North Pole. Ellsworth was convinced, likewise on the basis of his research, that it would be possible to make a series of landings in the unknown hinterland of Antarctica and take off again in safety. His plan was boldly based on this conviction and, like Nansen, he succeeded.

11

Whaler's Hobby

WHILE Byrd was probing into the continent from Little America, the Norwegians were pulling back the curtain from scattered sections of the coastline on the opposite side of Antarctica. Virtually all the Norwegian exploration was done under the auspices of the Christensen family of Sandefjord, whose whaling fleet combined the quest for new lands with the pursuit of the whale, much as the Enderby brothers a century earlier wedded exploration with sealing.

It was now possible to hunt down the faster species of whale from swift catchers equipped with gun-fired harpoons. Gigantic factory ships could process these monsters of the deep on the spot and in great numbers. This revived the whaling industry and focused it on Antarctic waters.

Christen Christensen of Sandefjord, Norway, was the leading sponsor of this revival and sent the first factory ships into the Antarctic seas. Christensen's son, Lars, better known than his father as a patron of Antarctic exploration, if only because his name now rests on the map of Antarctica alongside that of his wife, who accompanied him on all his voyages to the south.

The geographical exploration of the Christensens was

something of a hobby, but it was linked with a study of whale movements which was of great economic concern to the whaling fleets. It was evident that the whales migrated. One season they would be plentiful in a certain area, yet a year later whalers visiting the same waters would come back empty-handed.

In 1927 Lars Christensen bought a Norwegian sealer which he named the *Norvegia* and outfitted as a combined research and whaling vessel. For four successive seasons the *Norvegia* cruised in Antarctic waters. She was equipped with a seaplane in which Hjalmar Riiser-Larsen, an experienced polar pilot, flew across the pack and over the coast at a number of points in the sector south of Africa. The immense region bounded by these flights, six times the size of Norway, was named Queen Maud Land for the sovereign of Riiser-Larsen's homeland.

In 1935 a tanker of the Christensen fleet, the *Thorshavn,* made one of the most interesting discoveries of that period. On February 19, when the ship was 240 miles west of Mount Gauss, the coastal ice front was sighted and followed to the southwest. The next morning the skipper, Klarius Mikkelsen, found himself five miles off a rocky shore completely free of ice and snow. It was a labyrinth of bays, capes, and rocky islands—much like parts of the Maine coast but totally lacking in visible vegetation. A boat was placed in the water, and Mikkelsen embarked to make a landing with seven men and his wife, Caroline, who appears to have been the first woman to set foot on the Antarctic continent.

They landed in a small bay between two high promontories. Inland bare rocky hills rose as high as 1,000
feet.

The region has been named the Vestfold Hills for the
province of Norway which has sent men awhaling since
the Vikings decorated their ships with whalebone. The
great inland ice sheet was visible beyond these hills and
farther up the coast it broke through to the sea in a great
glacier. They cruised along about seventy-five miles of
ice-free shoreline with myriad harbors and penguin rookeries. The shore then ended in a bay and swung sharply
northwest to join the Lars Christensen Coast, discovered
by Mikkelsen four years earlier when he was skipper of
the whaler catcher *Torlyn*. He named the sector just explored Ingrid Christensen Land for the wife of the whaling magnate.

Christensen and his wife made four journeys from
Norway to the bottom of the world. "It is of course possible," he wrote, "for an owner of whaling ships to carry
on his business without ever having seen the whaling
grounds, but personally I like to familiarize myself on
the spot with the work which has engaged my interest,
my energies and my imagination for more than thirty
years."

Early in 1937, a series of flights were made from the
Thorshavn over the coastal areas named for Christensen
and his wife. She rode as a passenger on one of these
flights, and a guest of his wife, a Mrs. Rachlew, went on
another.

On January 25 the ship, with its echo-sounding gear,

found an extensive uncharted bank under the sea off this coast. "We gave it the name of The Four Ladies Bank after our four lady comrades of the voyage," Christensen said.

With this tribute to the fair sex ended a unique phase of Antarctic exploration.

12

Australia Looks South

THE LARGEST CLAIM in Antarctica has been made by Australia. It comprises almost half the land area of the continent, reaching unbroken from Queen Maud Land to New Zealand's Ross Dependency, except for the intervening sliver of France's Adélie Land. In its immensity the territory rivals the entire continent of Australia itself.

The man who enabled Australia to claim this region was Sir Douglas Mawson. Although born in England, he emigrated with his parents to Australia while a child and was trained there as a geologist. He is the only scientist who has led major expeditions to Antarctica, his period of activity there extending from early in the Heroic Era well into the Air Age.

Mawson's initiation to Antarctic exploration was with Shackleton's first expedition, when he was a member of the party that reached the Magnetic Pole. Soon after his return he organized his own venture, the Australian Antarctic Expedition, which departed from Tasmania as Scott and his men were nearing the Pole. Mawson's interest was in the sector south of Australia where no expedition had yet been based.

Riding in the *Aurora,* a former sealer, Mawson reached

the coast about 150 miles east of the point in Adélie Land where D'Urville had landed seventy-two years earlier, and followed the shoreline westward into what he called Commonwealth Bay, where a low, rocky cape enclosed a miniature harbor. This was called Cape Denison, and became Mawson's chief base.

Mawson appropriately named his account of this expedition "The Home of the Blizzard." Never had a weather station recorded winds such as those experienced at Cape Denison during the two winters that he was there. This was not a region of high coastal mountains. Rather, an unbroken ice sheet rose sharply inland to 3,000 feet and then more gradually to 7,000 feet and higher. The cold air of the Polar Plateau, seeking to reach lower altitudes, swept down over this steep slope like a great Niagara of wind, almost unceasing. The average velocity of the wind, twenty-four hours a day, for the entire month of May was 60.7 miles per hour. On May 24 Mawson estimated some of the gusts at nearly 200 miles per hour.

Much of the time it was hazardous to venture out of the hut. Those who did so before they learned how to handle themselves were snatched away by the wind and hurled into the snow. To keep their footing they had to wear ice-climbing crampons with one-and-one-half-inch spikes and lean into the wind until their heads were almost as low as their knees. If the blast stopped suddenly they fell on their faces.

The best-known journey of this expedition is that in which Mawson, Lieutenant B. E. S. Ninnis, and Dr. Xavier Mertz sought to sledge along the unexplored coast as far east as possible. In some respects it was a grimmer ordeal than that which, unknown to Mawson and his companions, had been endured by Scott's polar party a year earlier.

They set forth on November 10, 1912, with seventeen dogs and three sledges carrying 1,700 pounds. The first part of their route lay across two deep valleys through which glaciers flowed to the coast and far out to sea in the form of ice tongues. Mawson named these glaciers, both about thirty miles wide, for his two companions. They followed the shoreline for 300 miles without serious difficulty. On December 14 the sun was shining brightly and Mertz, a Swiss Alpinist and graduate of Bonn and Leipzig Universities, was in the lead, singing German student songs as he skied ahead. Behind him came Mawson, riding a sledge, and in the rear was Ninnis, an officer of the Royal Fusiliers, walking with his dog-team.

As had happened so many times, Mertz lifted his ski pole to warn them of a bridged crevasse across the trail. Ninnis apparently changed course to hit the crevasse at right angles. Mawson suddenly noticed Mertz looking anxiously to the rear and, turning himself, saw nothing but the boundless desert of snow. Ninnis, his dogs and sledge had vanished. He hurried back, finding to his horror a hole 11 feet wide and seemingly bottomless. On a ledge 150 feet down were two dogs. One was dead and the other lay moaning with its back broken. Near them hung what seemed to be part of a tent. For three hours Mawson and Mertz shouted into the depths of that terrible pit, but no reply other than a chill wind came to them from the abyss. The surface of the ice sheet was almost 2,000 feet above sea level at this point, and the cleft was probably many hundred feet deep.

It is possible that, had Ninnis been wearing skis, he would have been saved. It has since become standard practice for men on the Antarctic trail to travel by ski.

The lost sledge had carried all their dog food, their tent, and much of their provisions. There were no depots between them and their base, for they had planned to return by a more inland route. Their only hope was to travel as fast as possible on starvation rations.

For two weeks they raced with death, eating the dogs, one by one, feeding the others on leather straps and scraps of fur. They had covered more than half the distance back to Cape Denison when Mertz began to complain of severe pains in his abdomen. For two precious days they paused, and when they tried to advance on the third, less than five miles was covered. Again they stopped, and Mertz rested another two days.

On January 6 Mawson resorted to the desperate expedient of dragging Mertz on the sledge, even though his own strength was draining fast. They made but two and one-half miles, with one hundred miles still to go and only a few days' food left.

"Both our chances are going now," Mawson wrote in his diary. The implication was clear. If he abandoned his dying companion he might save himself, but he did not do so. The next day Mertz had a succession of fits and became delirious. At last he fell into what seemed a

103

deep sleep, and Mawson, himself exhausted from ministering to his friend, slipped into his sleeping bag. When he awoke Mertz was still motionless, and Mawson found that he was stiff in death.

He dug a shallow grave in the snow and for the second time read the burial service over one of his companions. A blizzard prevented his starting for a final effort to reach camp, and when he was at last able to set out, he found that his feet were in very bad condition. He had few illusions about being able to get back. "There is little chance of my reaching human aid alive," he noted in his trail log. He made no more than a few miles a day.

Part way across Mertz Glacier, the snow dropped out from beneath his feet and he plunged down until caught by the harness attached to his sledge. He hung fourteen feet down a crevasse and could feel that the sledge was creeping toward the edge. Once it slipped through the hole both he and the sledge would plunge into the abyss, but miraculously it stopped sliding.

Just as he climbed up to the edge of the crevasse the cornice gave way and he plunged down again. Still the sledge held, but it seemed useless to the weakened man to try again. The black hole below offered swift deliverance from his suffering. "... it would be but the work of a moment to slip from the harness, then all the pain and toil would be over," he wrote.

But the will to live returned and he tried again, wriggling out feet first. For an hour he lay on the snow surface to recover from this experience.

When he was still several days' march from the camp,

The icebreaker Northwind *leads the ships of* Operation Highjump *through comparatively loose pack.*

In a blizzard the huskies let themselves be drifted over. It helps keep them warm.→

Aerial view of "Bunger's Oasis" on the Knox Coast.

Science's answer to the chief Antarctic menace—a crevasse detector, the first used effectively in Antarctica. This led the party that blazed a trail to Byrd Station in 1956–1957.

Rivers of Antarctica are glaciers carrying the ice to the sea to become icebergs. This is the mightiest of charted glaciers—the Beardmore—as it begins its 100-mile descent through the Great Antarctic Horst.

↑ *U. S. Navy icebreakers carved a way into Marguerite Bay to enable Ronne's ship,* Port of Beaumont, *to escape.* Burton Island *tows her out.*

A snow bridge has fallen and disclosed a chasm large as a church. ↓

Two scientists drill into the Wilkes Land ice sheet with an ice auger to obtain a cross section of the annual layers of snow and ice. →

← *A scientist (Richard Cameron) takes temperature readings at various depths in an ice pit so narrow that he has to go in headfirst. This is in the previously untrod interior of Wilkes Land.*

A crane at Wilkes Station lowers the plastic dome over the radar used to track weather balloons to an elevation of twenty miles overhead. Note the prefabricated buildings are windowless. →

he saw a mound and on it found a bag of food left there only a few hours earlier by a party which was searching for him. It was enough to ensure his survival, and on February 8 he reached camp to find that the *Aurora* had departed only a few hours before to pick up the other part of the expedition. The ship had not evacuated Mawson's group as planned because of his absence. It meant another winter in Antarctica, but the ship had left ample provisions.

Mawson next returned to Antarctica in 1929, a few weeks after Byrd's flight over the South Pole. He used Scott's ship, the *Discovery*, which had been rigged to handle a seaplane. This enabled him to sketch in several gaps in the charted coastline, one stretch of which was named the Banzare Coast, for the initials of the expedition: The British, Australian, New Zealand Antarctic Research Expedition.

Antarctica is closer to Melbourne than Australia itself is wide, and Mawson wished to secure a generous slice of the land for his country. In this and the following season his men landed at five points around the perimeter of the continent to read formal proclamations, annexing "The Australian Antarctic Territory" in the name of King George V.

In 1947 the Australian government approved a plan to seek a site for a permanent station on the Antarctic mainland. Under the Department of External Affairs— Australia's foreign office—was organized the Australian National Antarctic Research Expeditions (ANARE), which since that time has conducted all that country's activities in Antarctica.

In January, 1954, Australia chartered the Danish ice ship *Kista Dan* and sent an expedition under Phillip Law to a point on the Antarctic coast almost 2,300 miles west of Mawson's original camp at Cape Denison. The base site, a pair of islands arranged in the shape of a horseshoe and attached to the mainland by the continental ice sheet, was named "Mawson."

In subsequent years a number of extended journeys have been made from this base. The first was one of the most terrifying trips in modern polar explorations. The party, led by Robert Dovers, who was in command of the base, set forth with two "weasels" in an attempt to reach Scullin Monolith, a towering rock on the coast 115 miles to the east. The weasel is a small amphibious vehicle developed by the United States for the island invasions of World War II. About the size of a jeep, it runs on tracks and is ideal for travel across snow and ice.

Dovers and his companions tried to make the trip in winter over the apron of sea ice attached to the coast, but a storm broke up the ice as they neared their goal and for many frantic hours they drove the vehicles from floe to floe in an attempt to reach shore. Each floe sank as the weight came onto it, and the Australians had to drive swiftly to the next. In tow behind the weasels were sled trailers in which they had been sleeping. Wild gusts of wind knocked these over; then other gusts righted them again. One trailer was demolished, and it was only by stubborn persistence and good luck that they got ashore with enough equipment and food to survive.

Other journeys were made along the coast to explore Edward VIII Bay, first seen from a distance in 1936 and named for the king whose brief reign ended that year in abdication. The Australians also explored a long range of massive peaks in the southeastern hinterland which they called the Prince Charles Mountains in honor of Queen Elizabeth's son.

13

Queen Maud Land

IN 1938, on the eve of World War II, the Germans made a bid to acquire a foothold in Antarctica. The Third Reich, under Hitler, was becoming increasingly active in whaling, and the sub-Antarctic seas were the only ones still abundant in whales.

Only two sectors of Antarctica had not been claimed by any government when the German expedition sailed from Hamburg in the *Schwabenland*. One was the region unofficially spoken for by Byrd and Ellsworth, and the other was what is now known as Queen Maud Land, whose coast had been explored at several points by the Norwegians. It was here that the Germans intended to stake out their claim.

On January 14, 1939, Norway proclaimed its sovereignty over all of Queen Maud Land. Five days later the *Schwabenland*, lying fifty miles off the western end of that region, launched the first German flight over Antarctica.

The German plan was to devote the season of 1938–1939 to aerial reconnaissance and mapping, returning to Antarctica the next year with a more substantial expedition. The exploration was to be carried out by two seaplanes of the Lufthansa airline launched from the 8,000-

ton catapult ship *Schwabenland*. The planes were to make a series of flights due south to their maximum safe range, returning twenty miles to the east of their outbound flight. The successive flight lines were to be so spaced that there would be a complete aerial photo coverage of the region with a 60 percent overlap. This was considered enough for rough mapping.

For seventeen days the ship worked eastward along the Queen Maud Land coast, sending seven long flights over the pack and well into the interior of the continent. The reward of these flights was the discovery of a magnificent series of mountain ranges parallel to the shoreline and from 100 to 200 miles inland from the coastal ice cliffs. The aerial photos taken show a belt of peaks about fifty miles wide, increasing in elevation to the east until not only the mountains themselves but a belt of terrain at the foot of their northern slopes is barren of snow and ice. This is especially true of the Wohlthat Massif, at the eastern extremity of the range, where two lakes nestle between sheer walls of mountain spurs. The lakes themselves are over 2,000 feet above sea level, bounded by steplike moraines sprinkled with melt-water ponds. Both lakes were frozen at the time the photographs were taken, and on the larger, which is about five miles wide, a captive iceberg was adrift. The magnificently stark panorama of the Wohlthat Massif has never been seen since its discovery.

To provide a basis for their claim, the Germans dropped a succession of spearlike markers every fifteen to twenty miles. On January 29 a special flight commanded by

Herrmann, the geographer, landed in a small bay in the ice shelf. A party climbed onto the ice and raised the Swastika a couple of hundred yards from the edge. "This is the outward sign that we Germans have trod this no-man's land and have claimed it for Greater Germany," Herrmann wrote.

In all, three such landings were made. The *Schwaben-land* received a cool reception when she met Norwegian whaling ships. "Our expedition," said Herrmann, "obviously is not in good odor with the Norwegians, who regard us as thieves and robbers, breaking into the South Polar region which, in their view, has been personally bestowed on them by the good Lord."

The portion of Queen Maud Land explored by the Germans was named by them Neu-Schwabenland. With the exception of Marie Byrd Land, it was by far the most extensive section of Antarctica to be surveyed from the air, and the photo-mapping techniques were a preview of those to be used, with greater refinement, after the war.

When the German expedition arrived home in April, its members were greeted by an honor guard of Storm Troopers and a message from Hitler that said: "Hearty congratulations on the successful carrying out of the tasks conferred on the expedition."

During the months that followed Hitler did not challenge the Norwegian claim to Queen Maud Land. He was preoccupied with other annexations and before long had occupied Norway itself. The war ruled out any further German expeditions to Antarctica.

While the war was at its height the next visit to Queen Maud Land had its genesis, although it did not reach Antarctica until 1950. It was to be the first expedition based ashore in that immense area, and, in contrast to the German operation, political motives were negligible in sending this new venture into the field. It was born in the mind of Hans Ahlmann, professor of geography at Stockholm, and its organizers were scientists, rather than adventurers.

Ahlmann, a leading authority on polar ice-cap formation, was intrigued by the German photographs of the Wohlthat Massif and a report of the Lufthansa fliers that the ice sheet 300 miles inland reached 13,700 feet in elevation. It was speculated that the blanket of ice weighing upon the heart of Antarctica might be over three miles thick.

An international expedition was planned by Norway, Britain, and Sweden. The areas of responsibility were subdivided down to the smallest detail. Britain, for example, was to furnish the aircraft and the tea, Norway a ship and the coffee, Sweden the houses and the toothpaste. John Giaever, administrative head of the Norwegian Polar Institute, was appointed leader. The expedition ship was the newly built sealer *Norsel,* and a snug little harbor in the ice shelf near Cape Norvegia was selected for their base, Maudheim.

In December a party led by Valter Schytt set forth to study the glaciers and ice sheet.

Heading eastward about seventy miles from the charted

coastline, it found two 750-foot hills which had been reported by the Germans and named Boreas and Passat for their two seaplanes. Two of the men went over to Passat to take some surveying observations.

"They had hardly set foot on solid ground," wrote Schytt, "before they discovered that in places the hill was bright with lichens of various colors—black and white, yellow and grey, orange and red—an absolute jungle for people who had seen no plant life whatsoever throughout the year of 1950. As well as lichens, there was green moss, almost luxuriant in growth and sometimes nearly an inch high."

While one member of the Glaciological Party took survey observations, the other sat and recorded the figures. As he did so he idly picked up a curious-looking stone and saw a tiny speck scurry across it. He unlimbered a magnifying glass and found that two species of spider-like creatures inhabited this utterly isolated pile of rock. One was red and very active; the other, brown and lethargic. Both were barely visible to the naked eye.

How had these tiny creatures come there? The scouring of the rock on the hills showed that, at the height of the Ice Age, they were completely engulfed. These midget spiders presumably were frozen solid and immobile many months of the year. Had they hibernated in rock clefts for the millenniums that their hill was inundated by ice, or had they somehow been transported there once the ice sheet receded?

Schytt and his companions were surprised to find that the ice level was not at present falling. The evidence in the rocks, he reported, indicated that the level had been stationary for at least several decades, for lichens were abundant even an inch or two above the snow. In other regions where the ice is in retreat, a belt of raw, recently exposed rock is visible at that level.

It had long been felt that the earth was warming up and that the Antarctic ice sheet was shrinking. This discovery raised doubts as to the universality of ice retreat.

A crisis of the second winter came in July when a lingering infection in the eye of Alan Reece, British geologist, became serious. It had been struck by a stone splinter when he was collecting specimens in the mountains. The expedition doctor, Ove Wilson, had never seen an eye operation, much less performed one. He was the thirty-year-old son of a Swedish-American figure-skating champion and had completed his internship only a few months before.

By means of the base radio he got in touch with one of his medical-school teachers, the eye specialist Sven Larsson at Lund University in Sweden. Larsson coached him in the examination and treatment of the eye and finally, in mid-July, on the basis of Dr. Wilson's reports, Larsson said the infected eye must be removed if the other was to be saved. Larsson, by radio, instructed Wilson in the proper technique, and Wilson in turn trained a staff of assistants by clandestine lectures late at night in the radio shack.

On July 21 the eye was removed. The operation took two hours and forty minutes but was successful, and the next summer the geologist was again wielding his hammer in the field.

During the expedition's final summer in Antarctica, its primary task was accomplished. This was to determine what sort of terrain lay beneath the ice sheet of Queen Maud Land. The technique, borrowed from oil-field prospectors, was to set off explosive charges on the surface of the ice and record the time interval until the echoes bounced back from the rocky floor underneath.

On October 18, 1951, the Seismic Party of three men set forth.

As they climbed toward the interior it became more and more difficult to detect echoes, and once they ascended the Neumayer Escarpment onto the Polar Plateau no echoes could be heard. They decided to stop where they were to try to devise some technique for obtaining echoes off the rock floor of the ice sheet.

For six days they tried every conceivable method, including the placement of the charge twenty-five feet in the air. At length, with the charges set forty feet down, they began to record faint echoes. After forty-six shots in this one location, they determined that the ice here was 6,375 feet deep. Their elevation was 8,800 feet, so the actual land beneath them was 2,425 feet above sea level. While still on the lofty plateau they measured an ice-sheet thickness of 7,800 feet—almost a mile and a half! The rock floor was only 600 feet above sea level.

After descending the Neumayer Escarpment, they found the Penck Trough, whose icy floor is a mile above the sea, to be a fiord which, if emptied of ice, would be partially filled with sea water. In all they crossed five such fiords before reaching the coast.

To the Norwegians it was especially thrilling to discover that, underneath its smooth white mantle, Queen Maud Land was deeply gouged by valleys and fiords. They quickly recognized that the coast of this remote region which they claimed for their own resembled that of Norway.

When the *Norsel* evacuated the expedition on January 15, 1952, she was laden down with scientific trophies of many sorts: a small mountain of geological specimens and, in the ship's refrigerator, a sealed box containing a moss-covered rock swarming with the tiny mites which they had found among the rocks of the inland mountains.

A small, scientifically minded expedition had done a thorough job on one section of Queen Maud Land, without seeking to perform feats that would bring them fame and glory. Beckoning like-minded expeditions are the Wohlthat Massif and many other untrod areas of special interest in Queen Maud Land and other parts of Antarctica.

14

United States Antarctic Service

IN 1939, for the first time in over 100 years, the United States decided to send a government expedition to Antarctica. By now the Antarctic continent had been split up like a pie, with all slices converging at the Pole. Each slice had been spoken for except that between 80° and 150° West, an area larger than Alaska, where Byrd and Ellsworth had made unofficial claims for the United States.

The American position was that claims of sovereignty over newly discovered lands, to be valid, must be followed by actual settlement of the territory. Hence the United States had made no official claim of its own and did not recognize those of any other nation.

The new American expedition, organized as the United States Antarctic Service, was to maintain permanent, or semipermanent, stations on the Antarctic continent. President Franklin D. Roosevelt appointed Byrd as commanding officer of the Service.

The primary objective of the expedition was to explore the region where a potential United States claim was strongest—specifically, to delineate the unknown coastline between Longitudes 78° and 148° West and to explore the hinterland behind the coast.

The expedition was to have two coastal bases at opposite ends of the sector to be claimed. The two bases would then send their planes and trail parties toward each other in an effort to chart the 1,700 miles of unknown coast which lay between. In addition, the Americans brought along the Snow Cruiser, a fabulous vehicle of shiplike dimensions designed to be an entire expedition on wheels. The Cruiser was large enough to span most Antarctic crevasses and thus, it was hoped, could strike out unhindered into the continent's hinterland. It had its own ski plane, which was to be launched every 250 miles to cover territory 300 miles to either side of the route.

In January, 1940, the expedition's two ships, *North Star* and *Bear,* sailed into the Bay of Whales. They found that pressure had so wrinkled the ice sheet at the old Little America site that the buildings were badly caved in. Hence a new location was staked out just south of Eleanor Bolling Bight for the expedition's West Base.

While the base was being set up Byrd headed east in the *Bear* in an effort to sail inside the pack along the coast of Marie Byrd Land. From what he had observed on earlier flights, offshore winds in late summer blew the pack away from the shoreline, leaving a channel of open water there. If a ship could once reach this channel, inside the pack, it could explore the coast at will.

In 1940, at least, this proved to be the case. The *Bear* rounded Cape Colbeck and sailed over 140 miles farther east than any ship ever had in this area.

Back at Little America the Snow Cruiser was unloaded,

but its heavy wheels, each weighing three tons, sank so deep into the snow that the vehicle could barely move. The Cruiser had to be abandoned as a vehicle of exploration and thus vanished its crew's dreams of scooting across the continental ice sheet, sliding down glaciers and acting as a mobile air base.

Shortly after noon on April 21 the sun set, not to reappear for 123 days. The men settled into a busy routine of scientific observations, as well as preparation and planning for the spring trail operations.

As the weeks wore on their life became more and more cavelike, for it grew so cold that those who tried to do heavy work outside came in coughing blood. The camp was completely buried. Main building, science building, machine shop, snow-walled aircraft hangars, food cache tunnels, and dog tunnels were all drifted over. The tunnels were so laid out that it was unnecessary to go outside except to read scientific instruments. The dog drivers, who had accumulated several hundred seal carcasses to feed their charges, improvised a "blubber house" where they melted down seal blubber, mixed it with dog food, and poured it into molds to freeze into one-pound blocks. These would be used next summer to feed dogteams on the trail.

On June 7, the forty-eighth day of the winter night, the men were lounging in the late evening, almost ready to turn in, when the door flew open and they heard the most terrible cry which can be uttered in the polar regions: "Fire!"

A tub of melted blubber had been ignited by the stove

in the blubber house, which was now a raging inferno. Beyond were the dog tunnels, with no outlet for the smoke. The first task was to prevent spread of the fire, but unless they could save the dogs their trail operations were doomed.

The men seized picks, axes, and shovels, and scrambled up the hatch into the night. Hastily a snow wall was thrown up in the tunnel between the blubber house and the main building while others on the surface tried to locate the roofs of the dog tunnels.

Probing picks finally broke through into a tunnel, but it was choked with acrid smoke. Two of the men dropped through the holes and soon were passing limp canine forms out to those on the surface.

Finally all of the dogs—almost sixty of them—were brought into the main building where the men lived. A roll call of man and beast showed that all were accounted for, and, though many were partially overcome, all of the dogs survived. Most remarkable of all, the bitch Dinah, who was in labor in the blubber house, had lost none of her puppies. Four had been born when the fire broke out, and after her rescue she whelped two more in the main building.

One of the expedition projects was the setting up of a satellite camp to make observations of the aurora simultaneously with Little America in an effort to determine the elevation of the displays. In the Arctic the height of this mobile and colorful phenomenon, known there as "Northern Lights," had been fixed at from 50 to 300 miles, but no such observations had been made in the Antarctic.

Not long after the midpoint in the winter night the auroral party set up its camp fifteen miles east of Little America. The observations were made with a theodolite on which a camera had been mounted. When a display was sighted radio contact was made with Little America. A point in the aurora pattern was selected and both stations photographed it. The readings on the theodolite then told the elevation and direction in which each camera had been pointed. It was hoped that this would make it possible to calculate with considerable accuracy the height of the display.

As the days passed the mercury sank. It reached 60° below zero, then 70° below. Finally it got down to —71.1°. It was so cold that, as the men stood peering into their instruments, their exhalations froze in midair with a sound like that of a newly opened soda bottle.

When the waxing moon began to drown out the aurora, the observation party, which had spent eight miserable days in the field, was brought back. To their horror they found that not a single photograph had come out. Apparently the extreme cold had slowed down the camera shutter. Finally, two weeks later, they repeated the venture. This time sixteen pairs of photos were obtained which they considered well enough matched to be used for triangulation of the aurora.

The hardships endured by the auroral party would have been unbearable a few months earlier, but a strange shifting of gears had taken place within them. It had long been suspected that the human body could adjust itself to climate. Two doctors, through blood tests and other checks, kept track of the changes that took place in the bodies of the expedition members from the time they left Boston until they had experienced the full Antarctic winter. The men stripped to undershirts and sat in the frigid tunnels while the doctors watched their blood pressure soar. They stood barefaced in subzero wind to see how long it took for the first frostbite to appear. In these men the entire function of the body had changed. Their metabolism was markedly higher. Even their skin structure had altered. Throughout the winter so much adrenalin was secreted by their glands that when it came to tooth-pulling even the slightest injection of adrenalin with novocaine produced adrenalin shock.

The doctors suspected that the large amount of adrenalin in their bodies made the men more touchy. Possibly it helped bring about the most terrible episode of the expedition. On the ninety-seventh day of the winter night it was noticed at dinner that one of the men was missing. A search of the camp confirmed the fears of his comrades. He had walked off, lightly clad, into a raging blizzard under circumstances which indicated he did not wish to return.

For more than two days the men sat gloomily in the camp, listening to the storm rage in the darkness outside, blaming themselves for every unkindness toward the missing man. He was given up for lost and his clothes had been packed when suddenly he reappeared, partially frozen but miraculously alive. The will to live had brought him to his senses and, by digging holes in the snow when exhausted, he had survived.

When spring came a series of trail parties set forth to explore the unclaimed lands to the east and enlarge man's scientific knowledge of that region. Except for the attempts to reach the Pole, no one had sledged the distances that were contemplated. The parties would have to cover 360 miles before arriving at the unexplored areas. One group was to try to reach a point 600 miles or more from the base.

To lay the depots of food and supplies for the trail parties, every form of transport was used—planes, a modified Army tank, a tractor, and dogteams. Three main depots were set up: one alongside the Rockefeller Mountains, 105 nautical miles to the east, known as 105 Depot; the second 130 miles farther out, at Mount Grace McKinley; and the third at Mount Rea, another 75 miles beyond that.

A seismic station was set up near 105 Depot atop a summit in the Rockefeller Mountains. Here a party was to record earth tremors for the first time in this region. The peak was named Mount Franklin for Benjamin Franklin, organizer of the American Philosophical Society, which had sponsored Antarctic scientific research as early as the Wilkes Expedition of 1838.

The remaining parties continued on toward their next goal, Mount Grace McKinley, climbing a succession of terraces onto the continental plateau. Here, when they had paused for a rest on November 2, the ice surface seemed to drop from beneath their feet and a thunderous noise resounded to the horizon in all directions. The dogs, with panic in their eyes, dashed back toward the team drivers, as though for protection. Apparently a great section of the ice sheet had subsided as it slipped off the shoulder of the continent.

As they penetrated into the unknown different groups of men fanned out to explore various regions. The Biological Party headed for the northernmost section of the Edsel Ford Ranges. Here, at Marujupu Peak, they found the richest plant life of the trip. The mountain had been named by Byrd for the children of Arthur Hays Sulzberger, publisher of *The New York Times*, and its name derived from the first letters of their names— Marian, Ruth, Judy, and Punch. Portions of its rock looked like the curly head of some sleeping giant, so dense was the covering of lichens.

Roped together, the members of the party clambered up the cliffs and painstakingly scraped lichens from the rocks and put them in match boxes for later study. In all, 3,000 specimens were brought back by this and other parties of East and West Bases. On the previous expedition, in 1934, Paul Siple had collected 94 species of lichen and other hardy plants, of which only 8 previously had been known. Jack Perkins, the expedition biologist, had reason to hope that many more plants would now be added to man's knowledge of the plant world.

The Geological Party explored the central part of the Edsel Ford Ranges, examining the mountains flanking both sides of an immense glacial valley which lay to the east of Mount Rea. They visited a total of fifty-nine peaks and brought back sledges full of rock specimens.

The Survey Party, traveling light with the best dogs,

sledged rapidly into the unknown regions to the east, where it was to survey the chief coastal mountains as far as a major peak, Mount Hal Flood, sighted from a distance by the last Byrd expedition. When its three men reached their destination, they found not one mountain but an eighty-mile escarpment whose highest peak seemed to be over 10,000 feet high.

This was the summit of their effort. They had sledged the equivalent of the distance from New York over the Allegheny Mountains to Pittsburgh and then on to Dayton.

By January 7, all the parties had returned to Little America. The Biological Party had traveled 725 miles in 72 days, the Geological Party 796 miles in 83 days, and the Survey Party approximately 1,200 miles in 83 days. Their sleds bore the fruit of their perilous labors: sacks of what they called their "hero rocks" gleaned from the many mountain ranges visited; scores of plants never before known to biologists; seismic records for a continuous period of 41 days, the first ever made in this part of the globe; bundles of newly drafted maps; and the notebooks essential not only to identify the specimens, but to give validity to the claim sheets placed at the uttermost reaches of their treks.

While the trail parties were in the field a number of flights were made from Little America.

Perhaps the most important was made in the Condor, a huge biplane. Flying east, along the coast discovered by Byrd the previous season, the fliers reached an immense gulf penetrating deep into the continent, beyond which rose a great white cone, slightly rounded at the summit like Mount Erebus. The peak, apparently a dormant volcano, is now known as Mount Siple.

Meanwhile, at the other end of the 1,700-mile stretch of coast, East Base had been established. En route in the *Bear,* Byrd had launched three important flights which produced the first sightings of this coast, comparable in length to that from Boston to Miami. He named the land seen on the first flight "Walgreen Coast" for the drugstore chain magnate who had helped equip this and his previous expedition. A second major discovery was a great promontory thrusting 100 miles out to sea, now known as Thurston Peninsula.

The site chosen for East Base was a low, rocky islet in Marguerite Bay on the coast of Palmer Peninsula which Byrd named Stonington Island for the Connecticut seaport from which Palmer sailed on his voyages of discovery to this part of Antarctica.

During the winter night, which was less severe than at Little America, the men of East Base took preliminary steps toward their two chief goals: the crossing of the peninsula to explore the Weddell coast to the east, and a long thrust to the southwest to search for the as yet unsighted lands which the United States hoped to claim.

The 800-mile stretch of Palmer Peninsula rises sheer from the sea with a mile-high backbone of rock and ice. The problem was to find a route across it to the other side. In July, while winter was still upon them, they discovered a route up the glacier that rose northeast to the crest of the peninsula and laid a supply depot at the top of the ice cap. Twice again, in the coming weeks, the members of the Weddell Coast Party struck out across the peninsula, laying caches farther along their prospective route and scouting a descent from the plateau down a long, deep glacier valley which they found on the other side.

Several near mishaps with the planes showed how blind they were to weather conditions on top of the plateau and beyond. On the other hand, from the depot which they had laid atop the ice cap, one could see the weather 100 miles out over the sea on both the Atlantic and Pacific sides of the peninsula. Thus was born the bold scheme of establishing a weather station at this "crow's nest" one mile higher than the camp on Stonington Island.

The weather men found that 86 percent of the gales came from the east and northeast. Often they found themselves above the clouds which blanketed Marguerite Bay and the camp far below them.

With their route across the peninsula established, the Weddell Coast Party set forth on November 19, provisioned for a two-month journey. Once over the peninsula, they sledged southward along the ice shelf, skirting the coastal promontories where they collected rock specimens. They found that the coast continued in a southerly direction, always flanked by mountains on the peninsula. By December they had reached 71° 51′ South, the first men to cross Palmer Peninsula and sledge down its eastern coast. To bear witness to their achievement they left claim sheets in cairns on the rock promontories which they visited and in a pyramid of snow blocks at their farthest south. They arrived back at the base on January 17 with twenty-two rock samples, extensive photographs and survey data, having covered 683 miles in fifty-nine days.

While the Weddell Coast Party was out, another trail team set forth to reach into the unclaimed region to the southwest. Seven men began the trek under the leadership of Finn Ronne, although only two—Ronne and Carl Eklund—were to make the long dash into the unknown.

After crossing the Wordie Ice Shelf, described by Ronne as the most dangerously crevassed area in Antarctica, they climbed gradually to 7,300 feet on the peninsular plateau. Here a survey party under J. Glenn Dyer headed toward the Eternity Range, and Ronne and Eklund struck out alone. They sledged south along the plateau until abeam of Batterbee Cache, which had been established by air 150 miles down George VI Sound, and descended a glacier to the depot. Fortified with provisions, they headed diagonally across the sound toward a tablelike mountain near the southeast corner of what was then called Alexander I Land.

This mountainous region was one of the first discoveries in Antarctica. Sighted by the Russian ships under Bellingshausen, it had always been regarded as part of the mainland, but in 1936 the British discovered George VI Sound, a great cleft between it and Palmer Peninsula. This led to speculation that Alexander I Land might, in fact, be an immense island.

As Ronne and Eklund set out across this ice-blanketed sound they were sledging into the unknown, for they had

127

passed the southernmost point reached by the Englishmen. Before them lay a gigantic highway of level ice that averaged twenty miles in width and ran on for hundreds of miles between parallel walls of mountains. At its end lay the answer to the riddle of Alexander I Land.

They pressed onward until, on December 17, they descended to what was obviously sea ice. Seal and penguin tracks were plentiful, and there were many leads of open sea water. Four days later they reached a cape on the southern coast of the sound. When they climbed to its 1,000-foot crest their hearts pounded with excitement, for beyond and to the north they saw a great sea all the way to the horizon. They had proven beyond doubt that Alexander I Land was in fact an island, linked to the mainland only by a floating ice shelf in a trough more than three times the length of Long Island Sound.

That night, on their regular radio contact with East Base, they reported their discovery but added that they had decided to turn back. They were still sixty miles short of the unclaimed region to the west, but, after nineteen days of sledging along the sound, time and food factors impelled their return. Their decision was a wise one, as events soon demonstrated.

With the warmer weather of advancing summer the surface of the sound was becoming slushy. Large meltwater lakes formed on top of the ice shelf and froze at night. Under the feet of the tugging dogs these surfaces became like broken glass. The trail was continuously stained with blood from the slashing of the dogs' feet.

They decided to dash for Batterbee Cache as fast as

possible, since there they would be able to rest while the feet of the dogs healed. After twelve grim days they reached the Cache. Ronne notified East Base that, of their fifteen dogs, only seven remained, and said they planned to rest two weeks before attempting to return. His radio went dead before this period was up and he could send a more reassuring report.

At East Base it was feared that the two men were in trouble, and a trail party under Richard Black, commander of the base, was organized to look for them. As Black's party was trekking southward they saw a dark object on a ridge ahead. Through their binoculars were clearly outlined a dogteam and two men.

"I have rarely experienced such a feeling of joy!" Black wrote. "Our search with all the uncertainty, the possibility of passing without contact, was ended! . . . We headed at full speed toward them . . . and were soon pumping hands and giving loud congratulations. Both Ronne and Eklund looked badly burned and very tired, but they certainly did not look to be in need of rescue. Eighty-four days and 1,200 miles of walking had made them as hard and tough as wolves."

It turned out that the dogs with Ronne and Eklund had improved very rapidly at Batterbee Cache, and after a ten-day rest they had set forth with a lightened load. Canvas shoes which they made for the dogs helped protect them from the jagged ice crystals until they climbed off the floor of the sound to the plateau, where the surface was soft. In eleven days of high-speed travel they covered 287 miles.

During their trip they had established twelve principal control stations, based on sun sights, from which they were able to plot the positions of 320 peaks and nunataks. Dyer's party had pinpointed another eleven control stations and had cut in fifty-eight mountains, including the 13,750-foot summit of Mount Andrew Jackson and the other chief peaks of the Eternity Range.

Meanwhile the men at East Base and West Base (Little America) had learned that the activities of the U. S. Antarctic Service were to be closed down. Europe was at war, and with all the resources of the United States focused on rearmament, Congress had not appropriated the money necessary to continue the Antarctic program. The idea of a permanent, or semipermanent, station on the continent had to be shelved for a later day.

The *Bear,* which had already evacuated the men from Little America, was unable, because of ice conditions, to come within sixty miles of the base at Stonington Island. The men had to be evacuated by air. The buildings were closed up and the instruments and specimens packed and labeled, with the request that the next visitor forward them to Washington.

The scientists of East Base and West Base returned to a country on the brink of war. In the view of Alton Wade, senior scientist of the group, they collected more scientific data than any previous expedition to that region, but much of it was never published. Most of the scientists were soon scattered around the world, applying their skills to military problems.

15

Through the Pack

AFTER WORLD WAR II the United States sent a new expedition to the Antarctic that was to dwarf any exploration venture in history. Thirteen ships and 4,700 men were engaged in *Operation Highjump*.

The expedition was divided into three groups. The Central Group was to push through the ice pack and establish a base and airfield at Little America. Transport planes would take off from the carrier *Philippine Sea* and fly across the pack to the newly established base, from which they would explore the interior of the continent. Eastern and Western Groups, each built around a seaplane tender, would work their way around the continent in opposite directions, sending their planes in to explore the coastal regions.

Admiral Byrd was named officer-in-charge of the "Antarctic Developments Project, 1947," and the ships and planes of the expedition were organized as Task Force 68 under Rear Admiral Richard H. Cruzen.

On December 30 the Central Group assembled off Scott Island. That forbidding black rock, crowned with a permanent ice cap, is the traditional starting point for those seeking to reach Little America. It lies on the International Date Line, which normally marks the easiest route through the pack. Rotating currents in the Ross Sea seem to sweep a clear path there, especially in late summer. At least nineteen ships have gone through without seeing any ice at all. The ships of *Highjump* were not to be so lucky.

The pack off Scott Island was far from open, but at the outset it appeared to be what Captain Thomas, commander of the Coast Guard icebreaker *Northwind,* called "sissy ice." Never before had the Navy sent its brittle-hulled steel ships through the Antarctic pack. Wooden ships had long been preferred for such work because, while they groaned and splintered under ice pressure, they did not rip. The *Titanic* disaster was the classic example of what ice could do to a steel ship.

Nevertheless it was decided to push south. Cruzen hoisted his two-star flag in the *Northwind* and headed into the pack, followed by the "attack cargo ships" *Merrick* and *Yancey,* then the *Mount Olympus,* and finally the submarine *Sennet.*

At first the ships rode on an even keel, steaming through a wonderland of blinding beauty. The pack was light, looking from the air as though huge, irregular pieces of white paper were floating on the sea. The *Northwind,* with its broad beam, left a wide channel through the ice down which the other vessels steamed, hardly grazing the floes.

This was "open" pack, but imperceptibly it began to become "close." The floes pressed back into the channel after each ship had passed.

To the south were solid fields of ice which resembled

desolate, snow-covered steppes. Several large icebergs could be seen. They are a hazard in the pack, for if a ship is caught in the ice it can be obliterated in a few minutes by a berg. The pack moves with the wind but the bergs, with their deep draft, may move in the opposite direction on the shoulders of a current, plowing through the pack like gigantic icebreakers.

Time after time one ship would hit a floe and stop. This would force the others to halt; whereupon the pack would flow back into the channel between ships and the whole procession would be stuck—every ship immovable except the *Northwind*. Then the icebreaker would peel off from the front, bully her way through the ice to the rear, and start up the column, passing each ship close aboard.

By working up the column in this manner she was able to get all ships moving again; but this routine had to be repeated so often that progress was miserably slow. Furthermore, it was becoming more and more obvious that a submarine in the pack was a fish out of water.

The *Sennet* had come along as part of the program to test naval units under polar conditions. She was equipped with special lighting gear to photograph the underside of floes, and was able, by means of supersonic devices, to take inverted soundings on the bottom of the ice to make sure she was a safe distance below it. There was interest in the underside of the pack, since some thought it so smooth that a submarine with runners on top and positive buoyancy could slide for miles under the polar ice.

Although no vital damage had yet been done to the

Sennet, the ice that was crowding up onto her bulbous sides was making her unmaneuverable. There was no choice but to have the *Northwind* tow her back outside the pack.

This operation proved to be as complex as herding two flocks of sheep through an area frequented by wolves. Because ships left alone in the ice pack are easy victims of pressure or drifting icebergs, it was decided to move the vessels into a pool of open water before taking the sub away. The *Northwind* then hauled the bow of the *Sennet* into a padded notch in her stern, designed for towing ships through the pack, and the two vessels headed north.

While the icebreaker was removing the submarine from the pack, disaster threatened the main body of ships. A shift in wind closed the leads of open water and ice fields hugged the ships' hulls in a vise. Then a squadron of fourteen icebergs was seen advancing toward them.

The *Mount Olympus* plotted the movement of the bergs by radar and found that one of them would pass directly through the place where the *Merrick* lay entrapped. The speed of the bergs through the pack was not great, but it was inexorable. The *Merrick* radioed that her berg was approaching at the rate of 100 yards every five minutes. As the bergs drew closer it became obvious that all three ships were in danger, for the movement of the bergs was erratic.

A series of urgent appeals for help was sent to Admiral Cruzen on the *Northwind,* while the ship captains resorted to every device they could think of to free their ships. The *Merrick* alternately dropped her anchors to crack the floes in front of her, while cargo booms hoisted heavy log fenders high over the ice on either side and let them drop. She managed to move about 160 yards ahead.

Nevertheless the *Merrick* disappeared behind the moving mountain of ice, and those on the *Mount Olympus* feared the worst. Then she reappeared on the other side of the berg, which had slipped between her and the *Yancey*, missing her by less than three shiplengths.

When Cruzen, on the northbound icebreaker, received the first appeals for assistance, he could not stop. The pack was so close and heavy that it was no place to leave a submarine alone. For several hours he pushed on north, while the cries for help from the south became increasingly urgent. Finally he found a pool of open water for the *Sennet,* and hastened back to aid the main body of ships.

As the icebreaker raced south, Richard H. Cruzen faced his hour of trial. He had learned that one of the flying boats of his Task Force was down somewhere in the Antarctic wastes with nine men, dead or alive. Judging by the messages he had received, three of his ships were in grave peril. He had been forced to abandon the submarine in a transient pool, near drifting bergs. Then word came that his son had been killed in an accident. When Commander James Mini, of the admiral's staff, saw the latter message, he consulted with Captain Thomas. They agreed that this was too severe a blow to heap upon their commander at such a time. Orders were issued to hold up this and the expected procession of condolence messages.

135

By the time the *Northwind* reached the other ships the situation had eased. She moved them to a new pool and again headed north. The pressure on Cruzen had eased somewhat. He turned to Captain Thomas on the bridge of the icebreaker and said, "Well, Tommy, things are looking rosy now. Let's go below for a spell."

Down in the cabin, Thomas recounted later, he drew a deep breath and said, "Admiral, sir, things are not altogether rosy. We have been keeping some bad news from you."

Commander Mini handed him the message reporting his son's death. After reading it the admiral said, "Excuse me, gentlemen, I want to be alone for a while—and thanks to you both for holding it. I really mean that."

It was hardly ten minutes, Thomas wrote later, before Cruzen was back with them, quietly discussing problems of the operation.

The icebreaker took the sub in tow again and by afternoon Scott Island was in sight. For the rest of the operation the *Sennet* stayed on the northern fringes of the pack, testing out her sound gear on the floes and icebergs. Her pressure hull was still sound, and she submerged a number of times near the outer edges of the pack without incident.

After regaining the main body of ships the *Northwind* scouted for a route through the ice but could find no easy passage. Finally a spell of bad weather loosened the pack, and from then on there were no serious difficulties with the ice. Within two days the ships were steaming down broad leads of open water and on January

14 they finally reached the southern fringes of the pack. Shortly after midnight the fabulous white wall of the Ross Ice Shelf was in sight. For myself and 1,500 other members of the expedition new to the Antarctic, the sight of these cliffs, level and extensive as the horizon itself, was an experience as moving as the landsman's first view of the sea.

Throughout the voyage south there had been discussion as to whether or not the Bay of Whales at Little America would be open. The bay was not a land feature at all. It was a cleft in the ice shelf whose size and shape changed from year to year. The two sides of the entrance were actually ice sheets which tended to flow toward each other at this point.

As the ships approached the Bay of Whales the *Northwind* scouted close to the ice front. Suddenly she vanished except for her masthead and radar screen, which could be seen moving briskly beyond the ice cliffs. She had found the entrance, completely invisible to the ships farther out.

When visited by Amundsen in 1911 the bay entrance was ten miles wide. When last seen in 1941 it was one and one-half miles wide, and now it had shrunk to 300 yards. Except near the entrance the entire bay was covered with heavy "bay ice"—the fruit of several seasons' freezing. To have a harbor where the ships could unload it was necessary to break out a large part of it.

The icebreaker *Northwind* moved in to do the job. As the task proceeded the bay became filled with eight-foot ice cubes. Within sixty-three hours an area was cleared one mile wide and two miles deep. Admiral Byrd later estimated that the *Northwind* had knocked loose 15,000,000 tons of bay ice.

The pack belt had been 600 miles wide, one of the heaviest on record for this sector. Without the power of the *Northwind* the ships could never have come through, nor could the Bay of Whales have been used for many weeks after arrival. The ships would have had to wait outside, hoping that eventually wind and waves would do what the *Northwind* did with such dispatch. This had been the debut of the modern icebreaker in Antarctica and a demonstration of what it could do.

16

Tragedy and Discovery

WHILE the Central Group was battling with the pack, the Eastern and Western Groups began sending their big flying boats aloft. Early on December 29 the first flight took off from alongside the *Pine Island* of the Eastern Group and headed for the mountainous coast of Marie Byrd Land. After ten hours in the air, following the shoreline westward with the mapping cameras in action, the Martin Mariner flying boat returned. Another flying boat was already in the air, and this one was readied for a second flight.

It took off with a flight crew, commanded by Lieutenant (jg) Ralph Paul LeBlanc, and the skipper of the *Pine Island,* Captain Henry Howard Caldwell, aboard. As the seaplane, designated "George One" for radio communications, neared the tip of Thurston Peninsula, it sent out a weather report:

CEILING 500 TO 1000 FEET SKY COMPLETELY OVERCAST OBJECTS NOT VISIBLE TWO MILES SNOW OR SLEET [barometric pressure] 29.32 INCHES WIND SOUTH 11 TO 16 KNOTS

This was not the kind of weather for flying over Antarctic terrain. The light, between a snowy landscape and a cloud blanket, could become so diffused that it cast no shadows—what polar fliers call a "white-out," when a snow-covered mountain may be invisible.

In forty-five minutes the plane reported it was at the plotted position 71°22′ South, 99°30′ West, only ten miles from the vaguely charted location of the coast. Then came silence. The plane had gas for a dozen hours or more in flight. It was only when this time drew to an end that those waiting on the *Pine Island* had to face the fact that it was down.

George Dufek, commander of the Eastern Group, decided that if the ceiling rose to 600 feet and visibility opened out to four miles he would put a plane in the water, hoping that by the time it was fueled and loaded the weather would be flyable. For six days the weather was so foul that even this modest requirement was never met.

Successive flight attempts then were made on January 5, 6, 7, 8, and 9, but were turned back by fog, blizzard, and low clouds. By this time the missing plane had been gone almost two weeks. Could any of its crew still be alive?

Finally, on January 11, the weather was fair and a plane headed south. Four hours later came the message:

MARINER GEORGE ONE BURNT WRECKAGE AND
ALIVE MEN AT 71-03 SOUTH 98-47 WEST

The search plane had been on the third leg of its flight, having flown inland over Thurston Peninsula and back, when the photographer of the plane crew spotted a column of smoke. Swooping down, they saw wreckage strewn on the ice sheet at the end of a long trail of plowed-up snow. About twenty-five miles away, several conical peaks poked up through the ice as though emerging above a smooth cloud layer. In the other direction was open water where a seaplane could land. It was less than ten miles from the group of wildly waving survivors, but they probably did not know it was there.

The plane commander scribbled a note telling them of the water and asking if they could make it on foot. If so they should form a circle, otherwise a straight line. He wrapped it around a sardine can and, swooping low, hurled it toward them. There was a huddle on the snow. Then, as reported in the account radioed to Admiral Cruzen, the men formed a circle, "joined hands, danced and stood on their heads."

The story of the crash was told by the survivors after their rescue and before they slipped into the deep sleep that comes with safety.

After sending what proved to be their final radio report, they neared the vicinity of the coast and climbed from 600 to 1,000 feet, which put them close under the overcast. The copilot, Lieutenant (jg) William H. Kearns, was flying the plane. Visibility worsened and the big flying boat punched through snow squalls until

Kearns thought he could see snow-covered land ahead with clouds right down to the mountaintops.

"Let's get the hell out of here," he said, and put the plane into a left turn. Apparently they lost altitude as they swung back toward the ship, for there was a sharp jolt. Kearns knew they must have hit a hump in the ice sheet and bounced back into flight again. He gunned the engines and tried to pull up and more to the left when the plane exploded, perhaps three seconds after the first impact.

The plane was torn apart and scattered across the ice cap. Almost all of its occupants were catapulted sprawling onto the snow. Kearns went up through the cockpit windshield and came to some distance from the plane.

The radioman, James Robbins, picked himself up from the snow. He was only stunned. Nearby William Warr, Aviation Machinist's Mate 2d Class, was also trying to get up. His back hurt, but he too was in fairly good shape.

They became aware of flames and screams from the wreckage. Kearns stumbled up to join them and they found LeBlanc dangling in his seat belt in the burning cockpit. The fuselage had been torn apart, so that they were able to clamber up, ignoring the fire and the danger of gasoline explosion. LeBlanc's head had apparently hit the throttle and he was only semiconscious. They dragged him out onto the snow and beat out the fire in his clothing with their gloved hands. For the heroism of this rescue all three men were later decorated.

The rear section of the plane, including the long tunnel leading to the tail, was still intact and lay well clear of the fire. The two able-bodied men, Robbins and Warr, put Kearns and LeBlanc inside and draped a parachute over the gaping hole.

Searching for other survivors, they found Ensign Maxwell Lopez, the navigator, and Wendell K. Hendersin, the radio operator, both dead. Nearby was Frederick Williams, Aviation Machinist's Mate 1st Class, who was mortally injured. He lived only about two hours.

Owen McCarty, Chief Photographer's Mate, lay unconscious in blood-stained snow with a deep, seven-inch gash in his head. They carried him to the tunnel, where he regained consciousness after about an hour.

Captain Caldwell had been carried off in the nose section when the plane exploded. He came to just before it hit the snow, and rising painfully, became aware of broken and loosened teeth.

All the survivors were suffering from shock and, overcome by stupor, they huddled in the tunnel section of the plane. They lost all track of time and later would not have known the date but for an eight-day clock in the cockpit which had miraculously kept running.

On the evening of the second day, Robbins, regaining his strength and appetite, aroused Warr and the two men headed for the galley in the forward section of the fuselage, looking for something to eat. They found some canned goods and brought back a can of apricots that was not frozen. Each man had two and one-half apricots, their first food after the crash.

Between long sleeps the first five days the survivors

poked in the snow around the wreckage for food. The medical supplies were almost all burned in the fire which crackled for an hour in the forward part of the wreckage, but 90 percent of the emergency rations, including 180 pounds of pemmican and 350 cans of lifeboat rations, had been scattered in the snow. They even found a stove, and for fuel were able to use aviation gas from one of the tanks which had not exploded.

Although their food supply was relatively plentiful, the men had no way of knowing how long it would be before they could be rescued, and they rationed themselves to two meals daily—breakfast at eight and dinner at six.

LeBlanc, the most seriously injured, was often delirious. His eyelids were burned so badly that his eyes were closed tight, and his face and hands were encrusted and swollen. On the seventh day some medical supplies were found and they began giving him doses of sulfadiazine tablets every four hours. Kearns rubbed cooking oil on his feet to try to keep up the circulation and prevent them from freezing.

As soon as they were able, Captain Caldwell conducted burial services for the three who had died, the first of their countrymen ever to perish on the Antarctic continent.

When the fog and storms cleared from time to time, the men found themselves in a sterile world of white. A few distant mountain peaks were the only bare land in sight. They scanned their surroundings and pored over a chart they had found in an attempt to establish their whereabouts. As their strength returned, some of the men reconnoitered their position, but the group remained at the scene of the crash, for they felt the plane would be a landmark for their rescuers.

Throughout their stay they tried to send messages giving their estimated position and spent hours cranking their emergency "Gibson Girl" radio transmitter. Their signals were never heard.

The castaways knew that there was no hope of rescue so long as the weather continued bad. Finally, on the twelfth day, a thin rift of blue appeared on the horizon and the sky cleared.

"The five of us spent most of the day around our hull opening hangout just enthusing all over about our good prospects and the perfect weather," Captain Caldwell recorded in his diary. "Supper—we had our usual stew but with beets rather than with beans tonight. Everyone ate heartily and between 7 and 8 turned in with the highest spirits to date."

Their elation proved to be justified, for the next morning Kearns heard the sound of a plane. There in the distance was a PBM Martin Mariner flying boat approaching. As Kearns described the scene, "Everyone shouted, and Bill Warr waved the brightest colored cloth he could find, an orange life-raft cover. Robbins fired the Very pistol; McCarty set off the smoke grenades."

To their dismay the plane flew over them and continued on its course. Throughout their stay the men had kept the snow brushed off the plane so that its dark body would stand out against the white landscape.

145

There was still a chance that the plane might pass nearby on its return, and the men were determined not to be overlooked a second time. Frantically they threw fragments of wood, rope, and parachutes into a rubber life raft and poured gasoline over it.

Two hours later they sighted the PBM again. They ignited their pyre and a column of black smoke soared 300 feet into the air. For a long moment the men watched anxiously. Then the plane dipped its wings, turned, and swooped toward them.

The little group on the snow placed LeBlanc on the sledge and set off in the direction indicated by the plane. The ten miles, tugging a heavy sled across the snow to open water where the seaplane could land, seemed interminable. It was only the prospect of warmth, food, and safety that drove them on. At every lurch of the sled LeBlanc winced from the agony of his raw back and open wounds.

Suddenly they heard the crack of a flare-throwing pistol and saw two men in the distance. The pair proved to be the rescue plane commander, Lieutenant Commander John D. Howell, and Richard Conger, Photographer's Mate 1st Class. Conger noted afterward that he was so overcome by emotion and by a compelling urge to see this pathetic group to safety that he forgot his calling. His camera hung forgotten by his side.

Howell and Conger hauled the sledge while the others stumbled along behind it. By now a fog was over them, and when they reached the rubber raft at the point where the two had landed they settled down to wait for the air to clear. Through the mist the deep thunder of the PBM engines rumbled as the big plane maneuvered to keep clear of drifting ice.

After about eight hours the fog lifted. They boarded the plane and headed back to the *Pine Island* where the medical officer, Lieutenant Commander H. E. Williamson, was waiting. The flying boat was hoisted, dripping, out of the sea and carefully lowered onto the deck. A stretcher brought out the blanket-covered figure of Le-Blanc. Next came Caldwell, who was rendered full honors by his ship. Caldwell saluted Admiral Dufek, the commander of the task group. Then they grasped hands. "Wasn't the slightest doubt you'd get us," Caldwell exclaimed.

When LeBlanc was received in sick bay, his burns were found to be grossly infected, with dry gangrene established in his feet. Two weeks after the rescue, when Le-Blanc arrived aboard the carrier *Philippine Sea*, the gangrene had moved four inches above one ankle and two inches above the other. Both legs had to be amputated below the knee before the ship returned home.

After the rescue the *Pine Island* sent further flights to explore the coastline between Thurston Peninsula and the region beyond Mount Siple, to the west. The entire coast was found to be about seventy miles farther south than previously believed, with patches of brown land exposed here and there.

By the time the Eastern Group finished its operations in this area, 600 miles of the coast had been photographed and the concept of the region had been radically altered. The photographs showed it to be a maze of islands, bays, and peninsulas, reminiscent of the inland passage in south-eastern Alaska. So deeply indented was the shoreline that the triple, horizon-to-horizon strips of photographs produced by the flights were not enough to show the extent of the bays. Open water lay along much of the coast, indicating that if a ship could once breach the pack she could sail with ease for some distance parallel to the shore.

The *Pine Island* worked eastward toward Palmer Peninsula and sent flights to photograph Alexander I Island, Charcot Island, and the southern part of Marguerite Bay. Her escort, the destroyer *Brownson,* tried in vain to land Dufek on the hitherto untrod shores of Charcot Island.

When the *Brownson* rejoined the *Pine Island* and was being refueled, Dufek climbed into a special steel chair to be carried back to his flagship. It was suspended from a trolley that ran on a wire strung between the ships and was pulled across the heaving water by another line.

When he was midway between the ships, the two hulls began rolling in opposite directions. With a sound like a pistol shot one line broke. Dufek plunged twenty-five feet into the icy water. Unless he could be rescued within eight or nine minutes his chances of survival would be slim. The destroyer heeled over in a sharp turn and its whaleboat picked up Dufek a few moments later.

The ship's doctor rushed him to the shower room and turned the water on hot. Dufek was held under the spray while his clothes were cut off. He began shivering like

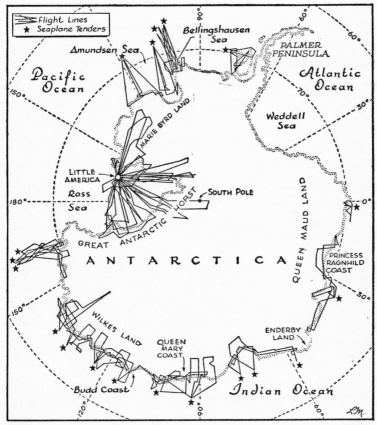

Flight lines from Pine Island, Currituck, *and Little America,*
Operation Highjump

149

a man with ague. "Turn it on hotter," he pleaded as the water poured down his frigid body. "If I did, it would burn your skin off," the doctor replied. Dufek could not feel the heat.

Expedition medical doctrine called for immersing such exposure cases in a bath of 115° to 120° if the man was unconscious, otherwise no more than 110°, since the higher temperature might be too painful to a conscious man. This procedure, which was developed in World War II, was a radical departure from the old belief that a frozen man should be warmed slowly.

Thanks to this treatment and the feat of the destroyer in rescuing him within eight minutes, Dufek suffered no permanent harm, although his hands pained him at night for several years afterward.

Soon after this incident, with winter approaching, Admiral Cruzen told Dufek to cease operations and head for a recreation port in South America. The men of the Eastern Group started for home, but they left behind them a unique memorial to the first Americans to die on the Antarctic continent. Atop the wing of the shattered plane on the ice cap of Thurston Peninsula was a message which the survivors had painted in anticipation of rescue:

"Lopez Hendersin Williams dead."

Under the wingtip the three men lay buried with only the snow and endless wind to watch over them.

17

A Virgin Coast Explored

THE SEAPLANES of the Western Group assaulted what was probably the longest unexplored coast in the world. Lying south of the Indian Ocean between Shackleton Ice Shelf and Adélie Land, it was comparable in length to the West Coast of the United States.

So far as was known, no human being had ever set foot there. A dotted line of the coast had been sketched in on the charts to indicate the general location of the shore, based on the assumed width of the pack or occasional humps of high ground sighted from a distance. This region, known as Wilkes Land, was within easy reach of the flying boats on the tender *Currituck*.

The initial photo-mapping flights over the mainland, which began on January 4, were made in the sector south of the Balleny Islands. The visibility on these flights was remarkable. Captain Charles Bond, commander of the Western Group, estimated that they could see 100 miles up the coast in each direction, spotting new islands and glaciers as they crossed the shoreline en route inland.

Mindful that a companion plane on the other side of the continent had crashed, the fliers kept careful track of open-water patches where emergency landings could be made. Lacking charts in this unexplored region, they made their own as they flew so that, in a pinch, they could retrace their steps. Glaciers, mountain passes, and other landmarks were sketched in. They studied the crevasse patterns in the flowing glaciers until they learned to tell which direction was "down."

On January 21 the Western Group began a series of long flights which, within less than six weeks, photographed a stretch of over 1,000 miles of virgin coastline. In addition, nine penetrations of more than 100 miles were made into the interior. The nature of this part of the continent, hidden from man's eyes since the dawn of the Ice Ages, began to become apparent.

Wherever seen, the interior of Wilkes Land was blanketed with a featureless ice sheet that ranged from 6,000 to 9,500 feet above sea level. No mountains were lofty enough to thrust their heads into the frigid winds above this white blanket, although valleys and ridges in the ice surface up to 100 miles inland gave a hint of rough terrain underneath. In contrast to other sectors of Antarctica there were no mountains along the coast.

The hinterland west of Wilkes Land presented a far different picture. On some of the deepest probes mountains could be seen, even farther inland, pushing up above the ice. The most impressive range explored lay in Queen Maud Land. This may prove to be one of the great mountain systems of the world. Its dimensions and extent are still unknown, but where photographed it rivaled in magnificence the mountains of South Victoria Land. The great peaks raised their rugged heads far above the ice sheet—as high as 13,000 feet, the fliers reported—damming up the polar ice until it spilled out through the passes in a series of mighty glaciers like those which empty into the Ross Ice Shelf.

The mountains lay 75 miles inland, extending 185 miles parallel to the coast, and presented tier upon tier of rock slopes free of snow. This range was an extension eastward of mountains discovered ten years earlier by a plane from one of Lars Christensen's shipborne expeditions. The jagged scenery resembled that of the Wohlthat Massif 200 miles farther west. The ranges are almost certainly parts of one great mountain system which runs the full length of Queen Maud Land and possibly much farther east. In the other direction the structure may connect with the Great Antarctic Horst. If so, it would be a chain comparable to the Rocky Mountains. The exploration of the next few years should tell us whether or not we have to add such a mountain system to those already charted on the maps of the world.

On February 2, 1947, one of the flying boats, commanded by Lieutenant W. R. Kreitzer, discovered a region which may be destined to play an important role in the history of Antarctica. He and his crewmates sighted a deep indentation in the coast cluttered with hundreds of rocks, peninsulas, and islands which, like the nearby mainland, were almost entirely free of snow. There were snug harbors and a few rocky beaches. The topography, like that of the Vestfold Hills, was reminiscent of the Maine coast, where an ice sheet also left its mark.

In the bare valleys and even on the humpy summits

were strange patches of black. Peering down through their binoculars, the fliers realized these were penguins —millions of them—sitting on their nests. Several miles inland a ridge of morainic rock ran parallel to the shore and was covered with an ice sheet almost to its summit, but the bare rock created enough heat so that a curtain of melt-water streams ran across the ice toward the barren shore. There must have been 100 square miles of snow-free terrain in sight.

Lieutenant Kreitzer reported when he returned that there was a large bay with what he considered an excellent spot for a landing field on its shore, and that the area would be easily accessible to ships once they were through the ice pack.

A second sensational discovery was the sighting of "Bunger's Oasis" a few days later. A PBM Mariner piloted by Lieutenant Commander David Eli Bunger was told to follow the eastern cliffs of Shackleton Ice Shelf in to the mainland. As he neared the coast about 110 miles from the open sea Bunger saw an astonishing sight—a great black patch in the world of white over which he was flying.

Approaching nearer, he could see that it was an area of at least 100 square miles of barren, rolling terrain splattered with lakes of all shapes, sizes, and colors. Brown conical hills rose up to 500 feet, and Bunger's men thought they saw small craters here and there. The lakes were pea green, dark blue, chocolate, and light green. Some of them seemed about 200 feet above sea level and several had beaches.

Two days later, on his next flight, Bunger landed on one of the oasis lakes. The men dipped their hands in the water and found it not unpleasantly cold. News of this discovery echoed throughout the world, for it was thought that this "oasis" might be due to volcanic heat in the ground.

Bunger's "Oasis" and Vincennes Bay, the site of the ice-free area discovered by Lieutenant Kreitzer, were revisited the following year by *Operation Windmill,* an expedition sent to obtain data for mapmaking purposes. *Windmill* was remarkable as the first expedition primarily dependent on helicopters to reach its goals.

Bunger was found to be an oval-shaped region of boulders, lakes, fiords, and rocky hills about thirty miles long and fifteen miles wide. There was no sign of subterranean heat. All the evidence indicated that shrinkage of the continental ice sheet had exposed the area.

The "oasis" was not inland, as had been supposed, but lay directly on the true coast. The long "lakes" proved to be fiords filled with sea water but isolated from the open sea by a great expanse of frozen ocean that was attached to the mainland.

It turned out to be a strangely lifeless and arid place. The only plant life found was some algae in the ponds and rivulets and a small moss attached to the pebbles in the tiny streams. Animals seemed to shun the region entirely, except at one point where fifty-five snow petrel nests were seen.

Vincennes Bay, on the other hand, was alive with seals and birds and the water teemed with plankton. It lay on a broad indentation in the coast with open water extending up to the shoreline. Unlike Bunger, there was no blanket of morainic material over the region. Clustered knobs of granite, smoothed by ice flow and wind-blasted snow, piled one upon the other 300 feet into the sky in grotesque patterns, as though bulbous entrails of the earth had burst forth from the depths.

The naval officers on *Operation Windmill* were enthusiastic about the potentialities of Vincennes Bay, as there were harbors snug enough to protect a ship from drifting bergs and shallow enough for anchoring.

The *Currituck,* on *Operation Highjump,* continued to work westward, its flights photographing the entire sector of Queen Maud Land from the Kemp to the Ingrid Christensen Coasts. One of the most valuable contributions of these flights was the light which they cast on the location of the true coastline. The radar altimeters enabled the airmen to keep track of the ice level beneath them, and they found that what in many areas had been charted by mariners as coastline was merely floating ice shelf. It was not until they had flown fifty to seventy-five miles inland that the ice surface beneath them began to rise, indicating that there was land underneath, rather than sea water. This was true along part of the Princess Astrid Coast and all of the Princess Ragnhild Coast in Queen Maud Land, forming a block of ice shelf which Bond estimated to be larger than the Shackleton Ice Shelf. This would make it one of the largest such formations in the world, exceeded only by the Ross Ice Shelf and possibly by the shelf at the head of the Weddell Sea.

Bond saw the increasingly frequent freezing of the ship's shadow—in the sea water—as an ominous sign that winter was approaching, and at the beginning of March ordered the three ships of the Western Group to point their bows toward Sydney.

18

First Air Base in Antarctica

THE CENTRAL GROUP, having battled its way through the pack, began setting up an air base at Little America. The pyramid-shaped tents, about sixty in all, were placed very far apart to ensure that, even in a hurricane-force wind, the base could not be wiped out by fire. An air strip was laid on the seaward side of the new tent city to receive the big planes from the aircraft carrier *Philippine Sea*.

Seven hundred miles to the north the carrier prepared to launch her six ski-equipped Douglas transport airplanes. Never had such large planes taken off from an aircraft carrier. Their wingspread was too wide for a normal take-off down the length of the flight deck. Instead a shortened run had to be made diagonally across the forward part of the deck. Once the aircraft were in the air they could not return, since the flight deck was too short and narrow.

On the evening of January 29 the ship's bugler sounded "flight quarters." The plane crews threw waterproof bags containing a complete change of clothing into the planes in case they made a wet forced landing in the pack. Dry clothes, under such circumstances, would make the difference between life and death.

Admiral Byrd climbed into the first plane on the line with Commander William M. Hawkes, who was to be in charge of the air unit at Little America, at the controls. Hawkes revved up his engines until they roared, then let go his brakes. At first the plane seemed to crawl, but abeam of the carrier's superstructure Hawkes opened his jato bottles, letting loose jet blasts that gave the plane a tremendous boost. It leaped forward like a greyhound and climbed steeply into the air with fifty feet of flight deck to spare. The second plane got off with equal ease, and the pair set forth together.

Hardly had they left the carrier when the needle on the radio compass in Hawkes' plane snapped around and pointed toward Little America. It had picked up impulses of the powerful beacon on the *Mount Olympus* coming to them across almost 700 miles of floating white wasteland.

They sighted the ice shelf from sixty miles away and, just six hours after taking off from the carrier, set down on the snow. The second plane came in seven minutes later.

As soon as word was received on the *Philippine Sea* that the first flights had arrived, the next two pairs were launched. All reached Little America safely, although the last plane had difficulty with both its radio and magnetic compass and was lost for several hours.

Before the first exploratory flights could take off, the expedition experienced its first blizzard. The 1,500 men of the Central Group had been lectured at length on the perils and problems of Antarctic blizzards. After two weeks in Little America they had begun to regard the descriptions as somewhat exaggerated. Then came their baptism of snow.

Chief Petty Officer Paul Saylor, an electronics technician, and one of his men set out from the Operations Hut for their midnight chow. It was broad daylight, even at that hour, but visibility was literally zero.

They passed one of the big planes, then the fuel depot with acres of oil drums rapidly being buried in the snow. The next landmark should have been a sign at the end of a tent row designating the corner of "Little America III Boulevard" and "Sledge-dog Avenue." They walked on and on, but saw neither street sign nor tents.

Two more men joined them, likewise lost and "a little bit panicky," Saylor said. Somewhere not very far away was the camp, with warm tents, companionship, and security. In all other directions lay the ice shelf, reaching unbroken for hundreds of miles, except to the north and west where cliffs fell to the sea.

Saylor lined the men up and rotated them like a tractor tread, ordering the rear man up the line and out ahead to the limit of visibility so that the column would move in a straight line. Thus they attempted to retrace their steps. Suddenly they heard the faint howl of a sledge dog. This guided them to "dogtown" where the huskies were chained in a circle. Most of the dogs had allowed themselves to be drifted over, but fortunately one was sitting up, howling into the blizzard. He was a much-patted creature for a few moments. Then, still using the scouting system, the four men covered the last hundred yards to the mess tent, picking up two more wanderers en route. Throughout the rest of the storm, the men ventured out only with bundles of trail flags, and, when the air cleared in the morning, the camp was a maze of criss-crossing lines of black flags.

There were about two dozen scientists with the expedition, half of them with the Central Group. Their studies ranged from sea-bottom slime to the ionosphere over 100 miles above the earth. Some were studying problems linked with polar warfare.

One team worked on the pulsation of the earth's magnetism at various frequencies in an effort to determine if the throbbing was simultaneous all over the world, and whether its causation lay in the sun, moon, or within the earth itself.

The shrunken state of the Bay of Whales stimulated a study of ice movement in that area. The bay, once several times as large as New York Harbor, had been squeezed until it was no wider than the East River. The two ice sheets which formed opposing capes at the entrance of the bay were being driven against each other. Paul Siple, who headed the Army's group of scientists, found that West Cape was moving north at the rate of 4.4 feet a day and East Cape was moving west at a constant daily rate of 4.37 feet. During our six-week stay in the bay the entrance narrowed by 170 feet, or about one-fifth of its total width.

In a report on his studies, Siple wrote: "Within four or five years the navigable portion of the bay will be completely compressed and by that time a great cataclysm will be close at hand. . . . When [it] occurs, the sites of Little America I, II, and III, as well as the more precarious tent camp of *Operation Highjump,* will float out to sea."

Siple's forecast proved to be astonishingly accurate when, eight years later, the *Atka* revisited this area and found that a cataclysm had taken place much as he predicted.

Fearing an early freeze of the pack, the ships of the Central Group departed from Little America on February 6, leaving 197 men at the base camp to conduct the exploration and be evacuated a few weeks later.

I was among this group, and it was with mixed feelings of excitement and isolation that we watched the ships go. We were left on our own, with nothing between ourselves and the blizzards except a single layer of canvas. The tents had been designed for use in a mild climate and, in fact, since most of our equipment was left over from the war, we were excellently equipped for life in the tropics. Each bunk was provided with mosquito netting. Our match boxes were inscribed with terse instructions to keep sleeves rolled down and take antimalarial pills regularly.

The first few days after the ships left, most of us were too busy making our tents livable to do much else. Since the tent pegs would not hold in the snow, the guy ropes were attached to four-foot extensions of the floor joists. We piled snow on the joists and built walls of snow blocks around the tents to break the wind. The snow, except on the very surface, was névé—what Byrd called "Ice Age

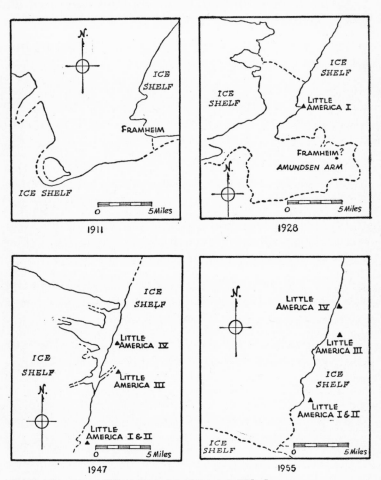

The changing Bay of Whales

snow"—and was similar in consistency to lump sugar. The blocks could be cut out with a flat-bladed shovel and were so compact that even when dropped only a corner would break off.

The biggest job was to construct an entrance tunnel that would keep out the wind. The most ingenious feature of our tunnel, in my view, was the fact that it had been dug out to a depth of six feet lower than the tent floor. This, I naïvely hoped, would drain the cold air from the tent. To provide access into the tent from this pit, I piled boxes into a rough approximation of steps.

When Admiral Byrd saw that our entrance was finished, he came to congratulate us and say a few friendly words. The tent flaps parted and Byrd's fur-encircled head appeared. "Hello, boys . . . ," he began, but could get no further, for the pile of boxes caved in and he sank out of sight. From then on the entrance was known as "Sullivan's Byrd Trap."

On February 13, 1947, the first flights were sent out from Little America. During the next fifty hours more unknown areas were sighted than had been seen in any such period in the history of exploration.

One of these flights, with Lieutenant George H. Anderson in command, flew southeast, seeking the extension of the Great Antarctic Horst, whose end no explorer had ever seen. It was a mountain system which began near Cape Adare, south of New Zealand, and ran for 1,500 miles along its charted route, then plunged into an unknown, unsighted region as large as Mexico.

As Anderson's plane winged over the Ross Ice Shelf, those aboard it grasped for the first time the magnitude of this continent. Hours of flying moved them hardly at all across their tan and white aerial chart. Then they saw the mountains and began their long climb into the breathless regions of the upper heavens. The range of peaks ahead was the Horlick Mountains. They flew to the right of it and saw a mountain wall with cloud banks hugging its foundations. The new range was a great escarpment of reddish rock which towered above them, even though they were flying at 13,000 feet. It was a mighty battlement, not a jagged range of peaks and passes, and must have been the continuation of the Horst.

They had been flying at 13,000 feet for forty-five minutes when, the copilot said afterward, the landscape suddenly turned pink and he began to have that "I-don't-care" feeling.

Anoxia—the effect of flying too high without oxygen—was to be a problem on many of the flights. The six planes had all been equipped with oxygen apparatus for high flying, but it was removed, on the carrier, to lighten them for the flight into Little America. The effect of anoxia is to cause a change in personality, producing irresponsibility, irritability, and clumsiness—qualities that can be fatal in the air.

Anderson swung the plane around and headed back. They had reached 200 miles farther east than any previous explorer in this region. At their turning point the mountains of the Horst were lofty and continued as far as could be seen in the direction of the known mountains of Queen

Maud Land, 700 miles away. Since no one could even guess what happened to them in the vast intervening hinterland, we described them as "The Endless Mountains." Presumably they were those glimpsed by Amundsen when only 138 miles from the Pole. He wrote:

"Summit after summit the range extended to the southeast, until it gradually disappeared; but to judge from the atmosphere, it was continued beyond our range of vision in the same direction. That this chain traverses the Antarctic continent I therefore consider beyond a doubt."

While Anderson's flight was seeking to extend the known portion of the Horst to the southeast, two other Douglas transports set forth to look behind the Horst in the southwest. Except where Scott and Shackleton had struck for the Pole via the Beardmore Glacier, no one had entered these mountains or flown over them.

The two aircraft headed for Shackleton Glacier. Flying up opposite sides of it, the airmen gazed down in amazement on what appeared to be a superhighway laid on top of the ice. It was made up of silt, gravel, or rocks and must have been 300 yards wide. Running brooks glistened in the center or along its margins, their course following that of the glacier. The phenomenon is known as a medial moraine.

The plane reached the summit, and as the mountains fell behind the fliers the smooth plateau rose gradually. They were at 13,000 feet and their radar altimeter, bouncing impulses off the surface below them, registered an altitude of only 1,500 feet. This showed that the ice sheet here was about 11,500 feet above sea level, high enough to bury without trace all the mountains of the eastern United States.

They had crossed the plateau route of Scott and Shackleton and had gone 140 miles beyond, toward the Indian Ocean. The scene was like that at the Pole—a lofty, featureless ice sheet. They turned and headed back along the Beardmore Glacier. This Mississippi of ice rivers was, until the discoveries of the next few days, the largest known, being 100 miles long and an average of 12 miles wide. The men looked down in awe, not only at the scenery, but at the thought that they were the first to descend the Beardmore since Scott and his companions dragged their dwindling supplies down its massed crevasses and ice falls, doomed to die one by one before they could reach their base.

When these planes returned, two more flights took off, this time for the east. In the region immediately south of the Executive Committee Range they saw an immense conical peak which seemed to be an old volcano. Although the planes were flying at their maximum permitted altitude, the great peak towered so high that they could fly only along its base. Thousands of feet above them soared the rock and snow slopes. Paul Siple, who was the navigator on the flight, estimated that the peak was about 20,000 feet high—loftier than any of the Alps or Rockies. If the new peak is that high, it will rival Mount McKinley, loftiest in North America, and will be by far the highest so far discovered on the Antarctic continent.

167

A second peak, estimated at 15,000 feet, was sighted nearby. The fact that these new mountains, like Mounts Siple and Sidley nearer the coast, all appear to be volcanic cones suggests that they may be part of the system of volcanoes girdling the Pacific from the Far East through the Aleutians, California, and Mexico to the Andes and Antarctica.

On February 15, Byrd decided to try for his other primary goal, the unsighted heartland of Antarctica beyond the Pole. Over the Pole Byrd dropped a box containing the flags of all members of the United Nations, and the two planes then flew eighty miles beyond for a glimpse into the unknown. The air was crystal clear and they were about 2,500 feet above the surface. All that could be seen in any direction was the flat white crust of the ice sheet. "If there was anything to see we could see 150 miles," Byrd said after his return.

The next flight, which went west into the hitherto unknown "backyard" of South Victoria Land, produced one of the chief discoveries of *Operation Highjump*. It was a mighty glacier, which Byrd believes may be the largest known, formed by three ice rivers which flow together. The glacier, which was sighted alongside Mount Markham, probably empties into the Ross Ice Shelf via Shackleton Inlet.

Three days later Hawkes took off again toward Victoria Land. Near Ferrar Glacier the plane circled and its crew gazed down on a fantastic scene. It resembled the Grand Canyon of the Colorado, both because of its bricklike reds and because of its formation, for this, the geologists later decided, was a plateau dissected by flowing ice or water into a succession of deep gorges.

A number of the gorges were all or partly free of snow. It was in this area that members of the Scott expeditions discovered eight or nine "dry" valleys. Now, with man's eyes lifted into the skies, it was possible to see even more and to record the complete picture of this strange region. While Hawkes photographed the dry valleys from their upper or western end, his companion plane shot them from their lower or eastern end. The resulting pictures show the Ice Age retreating. For the first time one can see dramatic evidence that water erosion has begun again on this continent. This is shown in the photographs of one valley where streams of melt-water have created some of the water-molded features of more temperate lands. The streams have cut miniature river valleys and have deposited fans of alluvial silt on the valley floor. A delta is being laid down where the main stream empties into a lake. The soil, swept away by millenniums of ice flow, is being replaced. If, on foot or by helicopter, a geologist ever reaches this gorge, by examination of these alluvial fans and deltas he may be able to estimate how long ago the ice quit this valley and the water went to work.

Another exploratory flight of an entirely different nature was made that same day. It was a survey by airborne magnetometer, an instrument that can detect how far it is above a layer of metamorphic or igneous rock by recording the magnetic tug of those rocks. James R. Balsley of the U. S. Geological Survey had accompanied the Central

Group to test this device over the Antarctic Ice Sheet. I accompanied him on this hop.

We headed for the mainland and neared the Alexandra Mountains. As we passed La Gorce Peak, whose sharp, canted crag resembles the Matterhorn in Switzerland, I noticed that Balsley was running excitedly back and forth, checking his instruments, looking out at the mountains, then back to his dials. Once we had passed the peak he paused to explain his excitement. No human being had ever set foot on the terrain below us, but Amundsen's expedition had brought back rocks from Scott Nunataks, thirty miles to the northwest, and the Byrd expeditions had collected specimens from the Rockefeller Mountains, forty miles to the southwest. In both cases the mountains were found to be made of rocks which had been "cooked" in the earth's furnace—granites and metamorphosed sediments—most of which are magnetic. Yet Balsley learned from his instrument that La Gorce Peak, midway between these two mountain groups, was nonmagnetic and was probably of virgin sedimentary rock.

No such formation had yet been visited in Marie Byrd Land, which means that we know little of the history of that region, since the fossils that record it are found only in sedimentary rocks. It may therefore prove worthwhile to visit La Gorce Peak.

One of the last exploratory flights, on its return, reported that west of Discovery Inlet 90 percent of the Ross Sea had frozen over. Admiral Cruzen decided the time had come to evacuate Little America. The nine planes at the base had to be left behind, but it was hoped they might be used by some future expedition.

During the long voyage home, aerial photos of the Central Group were developed and a preliminary study made. The photo interpreter tried to reconcile the pictures with the flight paths reported by the pilots. He ran into a succession of problems. When photographs from the four long flights to the southeast were examined, he found that two flights, plotted far apart by the navigators, were shown by the photographs to have followed almost identical routes. The other two flights, thought to have flown the same track, produced photos of completely different areas.

This illustrated the weaknesses of aerial navigation and photo mapping in the Antarctic. The plane crews had no aids to navigation except fleeting glimpses of the sun and compasses which behaved erratically so near the Pole. At the far end of a 700-mile flight the "dead reckoning" position of the most skillful navigator could be off as much as 100 miles.

The photography of the Central Group was therefore chiefly useful as "reconnaissance" rather than for mapping. The coastal photography of the seaplanes from the Eastern and Western Groups, on the other hand, was more readily applicable to mapmaking because the landmarks that appeared in the pictures were more accessible to ground parties of later expeditions. Once these "ground control points" could be pinpointed by sun sights, entire strips of photographs could be oriented.

Despite these limitations it was felt that *Operation Highjump* had been a success. The three groups of the expedition had made a total of 101 flights and discovered an area estimated at 350,000 square miles. They had taken some 70,000 photographs.

At least eighteen mountain ranges or groups of mountains and ten or more individual mountains of importance were discovered. "The new maps," said the Navy report, "will show numerous glaciers, nunataks and skerries along the coastline as well as thirteen newly discovered (or enlarged) bays and nine capes."

The estimate of the newly discovered land was equal to the combined areas of France and Germany. When the ships sailed home only one major stretch of coast still had not been sighted by man—that south of the Weddell Sea.

19

Struggle for Palmer Peninsula

DURING THE NIGHT of January 13, 1941, two of Lars Christensen's gigantic factory ships, *Ole Wegger* and *Solglimt,* wallowed in the sea north of Queen Maud Land. They were moored together, with the water about their ungainly hulls full of bloated whales brought in by their catchers. The crews had put in a hard day's work processing whales. Not a soul was stirring on deck.

A fog which had hugged the ocean lifted close to midnight, and a strange ship appeared close by. She placed boats in the water which approached the Norwegian vessels. Heavily armed sailors scrambled across the slippery whale carcasses and up a ladder which hung conveniently over the side of *Ole Wegger.*

A few moments later, the skipper of the factory ship heard his cabin door open. He sensed something was wrong and reached toward his jacket, hanging over a chair. A boot kicked the chair out of reach.

"Take it easy, Captain," said a voice in the half-light. "Your ship has been occupied by a German raider-commando." The German officer removed a heavy wallet and a pistol from the captain's jacket, then returned it.

"Anderson, captain of this ship," said the Norwegian.

"Bach," said the German lieutenant with a military bow. "Forgive the disturbance, Captain. It is war."

The remainder of Bach's men had occupied the key points on *Ole Wegger*. Another prize crew had taken over *Solglimt*. Before the day was out a third factory ship, *Pelagos*, was likewise seized, and a German officer who spoke Norwegian went to the whaler's radio and casually summoned all other catchers to return. A few escaped, but in twenty-four hours the German raider *Pinguin* had captured three factory ships and eleven catchers, with a grand total of 40,000 tons—a large part of the Norwegian whaling fleet.

War had come to Antarctica, and henceforth the continent was to figure in the strategic thinking of the great powers. With sub-Antarctic waters as a refuge the German raiders sank or captured several hundred thousand tons of Allied shipping. The British knew that the raiders were basing somewhere in the Antarctic. British warships conducted searches of the Kerguelen Islands and the abandoned whaling station on Deception Island, near the tip of Palmer Peninsula. Here they found evidence that an Argentine naval vessel had visited the island a year earlier, leaving an announcement that Argentina had taken possession of an area which included Palmer Peninsula.

The British feared that a pro-German Argentine government might gain control of both sides of the passage linking the Atlantic and Pacific. Although hard pressed on many fronts, Britain decided to send a small military force to Palmer Peninsula.

The result was *Operation Tabarin,* a secret plan to set up bases on Deception Island and elsewhere on Palmer Peninsula.

Ever since the days when, as "Yankee Harbor," it had been the Antarctic home port for sealers from Stonington and other New England ports, Deception Island had proved an ideal—though not always peaceful—anchorage for visitors to Antarctica. The restless forces in the heart of the earth never let the mariner forget that this was once the crater of a volcano. The hot sand on its beaches and even the water along the shoreline steamed in the frigid air. In 1921 the water is said to have boiled across half the harbor, taking paint off the hulls of ships anchored there.

The British placed one base at the whaling station in Whalers Bay, near the narrow cleft through which ships sail in and out of the crater, and the second on Wiencke Island, 220 miles farther down the peninsula. A year later, a third base was set up at Hope Bay. During the four-year life of the latter station, nine major sledge journeys were made over a total distance of some 3,100 miles.

On November 4, 1948, four of the seven men living at Eagle House, as the hut at Hope Bay was called, started out with their dogteams to make a series of "astrofixes," establishing the positions of landmarks on the northwest coast of Palmer Peninsula. Four days later Dr. W. J. L. Sladen, the base medical officer, went to visit an immense rookery on the slopes above the bay, where an estimated 54,000 Adélie penguins had built their nests.

Behind at Eagle House, presumably asleep, he left two

of his "guinea pigs"—the meteorologist Burd and the geologist Green. Dr. Sladen had been studying the bacteria in the noses and throats of his companions to try to determine the "purifying" effects of life in Antarctica.

On his return from the long hike around the bay he saw to his horror that smoke and flames were pouring from Eagle House. He ran as fast as he could across the rocky slopes, but by the time he got there the house was a raging inferno. He could not even get near it.

When the fire burned itself out he was alone in the most desolate region on earth. Both his companions were dead, and the fruit of his experiments, as well as all the records of geological and survey work on the season's sledging journeys, had been destroyed. Fortunately, part of their supplies had been stored elsewhere.

The four men on the trail wondered why they could not contact their base by radio and finally returned. With their trail radio they broadcast an appeal for help. Three months later the FIDS ship *John Biscoe* arrived to rescue them. The station at Hope Bay was evacuated and not rebuilt until 1952.

When the British returned in that year they found an Argentine party already installed there. The Argentine commander informed them that he was under orders "to prevent you from building a base here, using force if necessary." Shortly thereafter, a few machine-gun bursts were fired over the heads of the British shore parties and rifle-bearing Argentines surrounded them and sent them back to their ship.

In response to a vehement British protest, the Argentine government declared it was all a mistake, and the British ship *John Biscoe* proceeded to unload.

Meanwhile, early in 1946, another British party had set up a base on Stonington Island, the site of the 1940 U. S. Antarctic Service base.

The following year a stubby little motor vessel swung into the bay off Stonington Island, loaded down with aircraft, weasels, sledge dogs, and Americans. It was the expedition led by Finn Ronne, which had come to reoccupy the American base, a mere two hundred yards from the new British station.

Compared to the Byrd expeditions, this one had been organized on the proverbial shoestring, with only about $50,000 cash available to purchase supplies. The Navy had loaned Ronne a vessel, the *Port of Beaumont*, the Army had made available two weasels, and the Air Force three planes. To save money, no professional sailors had been signed on. The expedition members sailed the ship themselves.

When the British came to greet Ronne, they were amazed to see women in his party. For the first time explorers had brought their wives to winter with them in the Antarctic. Two ladies were aboard, Mrs. Darlington, wife of Harry Darlington, and Mrs. Ronne.

The British embassy in Washington had tried to discourage Ronne from returning to Stonington Island, reminding him that this location was within the sector claimed by Britain. Ronne, however, had little choice, as his funds were so limited he could not build a new base. For a time after his arrival at Stonington Island relations between the Americans and the British were distinctly cool, but as winter approached the interdependence of the two groups became obvious and their differences were submerged.

Ronne and Major K. S. Pierce Butler, the British commander, decided on joint British-American field operations for the next summer.

Their first step was to establish a weather station on the summit of the peninsular ice cap, as the Americans had done in 1940. Dodson, the assistant geologist, and Peterson, the physicist, were the initial team to man it.

One evening shortly thereafter, as the Stonington Island personnel were viewing a motion picture, the audience became aware that a man had pushed into the room and was trying to pick out Ronne in the darkness. It was Dodson, who reported that Peterson was down a crevasse. Their tent had torn and become unlivable, he said, and they had decided to return to base. Unwisely they removed their skis.

A British-American rescue party hurried up the glacier and lowered Butson, the British doctor, deep into the abyss. "Here he is," he called. "He's alive! Very much so, in fact. He's talking!" Peterson was 110 feet down, wedged head downward. His shouts, perforce directed down, had been lost in the depths. Although he had been in the crevasse for almost twelve hours, upside down, he recovered fully.

The program agreed upon between the British and American expeditions provided for an American geological trip to Alexander I Island, and for a joint British-

American sledging trip across the peninsula and down its east coast as far as possible. The British were to name any features discovered north of Mount Tricorn, and the Americans would name those south of there. Ronne's planes were to provide air support which they hoped would make it possible to go far beyond the point reached by the men from East Base six years earlier.

The first step was to airlift a depot and weather station to Cape Keeler, almost directly opposite the base on the eastern side of the peninsula. During this operation the mosquito-like Auster plane used by the British disappeared, and only after a week of searching were its three occupants located on the west coast of the peninsula. They had been caught in a blizzard while flying through the mountains. On reaching the west coast they had been unsure of their position and had landed on the sea ice. In the poor visibility, one ski struck a lump of ice and the plane flipped over on its back. No one was hurt, but they found themselves eighty miles south of the base with little trail equipment. They did not even have skis or snowshoes, and underneath a thin, breakable crust the sea ice was covered with a deep layer of slush. At every step they went in up to their knees. Their clothes were soon soaked with salty water, which bit into their flesh in the icy wind. They rationed themselves to a mere three ounces of pemmican a day until, shortly before their rescue, they saw a seal and killed it with an ice ax. They were eating it when found, but each man had lost twenty pounds.

The British-American team reached Bowman Peninsula at the southwest corner of the Weddell Sea, over 200 miles beyond the point achieved by the previous American expedition. Since a British party from Hope Bay was sledging down the east coast to Stonington Island, it meant that in one season sledge parties had traveled the entire east coast of Palmer Peninsula. The joint party returned after covering 1,180 miles in 106 days. It was a memorable journey, not only for the distance covered and the constant use of air support, but also because of its "international" composition.

While the trail parties were in the field, Ronne made three important long-range flights. In the first, he flew in his Beechcraft 450 miles south along the Weddell Sea coast to the vicinity of Bowman Peninsula. Here he landed and refueled from gasoline carried by his accompanying plane, the *Norseman*. The Beechcraft continued on alone, following the Palmer Peninsula mountain range "wherever it might lead," for no one knew what happened to it, once it plunged into the Antarctic hinterland. To Ronne's amazement, instead of following the curve of Palmer Peninsula toward Queen Maud Land, the mountain chain reversed its curve and swung toward the southwest and Marie Byrd Land.

When he reached the terminal peak of the visible mountains, which he named Mount Hassage, he swung back to the ice-shelf front and followed it for over 200 miles toward Vahsel Bay. Ronne found the shoreline to be a straight ice front, thus establishing the south coast of the Weddell Sea to be an ice-shelf "barrier" similar to that which bounds the southern shore of the Ross Sea.

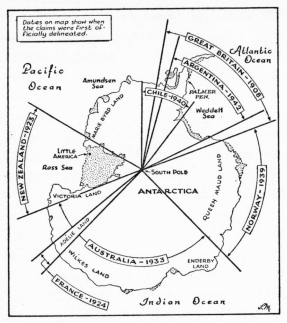

Dates on map show when the claims were first of-ficially delineated.

Pacific Ocean

Amundsen Sea

GREAT BRITAIN - 1908

Atlantic Ocean

ARGENTINA - 1942

CHILE - 1940

PALMER PEN.

MARIE BYRD LAND

Weddell Sea

NEW ZEALAND - 1923

LITTLE AMERICA

Ross Sea

SOUTH POLE

ANTARCTICA

QUEEN MAUD LAND

NORWAY - 1939

VICTORIA LAND

ADÉLIE LAND

WILKES LAND

AUSTRALIA - 1933

ENDERBY LAND

FRANCE - 1924

Indian Ocean

National claims in the Antarctic

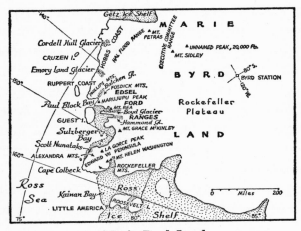

Getz Ice Shelf.

M A R I E

HOBBS COAST

MT. PETRAS

EXECUTIVE COMMITTEE RANGE

Cordell Hull Glacier

CRUZEN I.

VAL FLOOD RANGE

UNNAMED PEAK, 20,000 Ft.

MT. SIDLEY

Emory Land Glacier

PHILLIPS MTS.

Balchen Gl.

B Y R D

80° S

BYRD STATION

120° W.

RUPPERT COAST

FOSDICK MTS.

EDSEL

Rockefeller Plateau

Paul Block Bay

MARUJUPU PEAK

FORD

MT. REA

GUEST I.

RANGES

Boyd Glacier

Hammond Gl.

MT. GRACE McKINLEY

L A N D

Sulzberger Bay

Scott Nunataks

LA GORCE PEAK

EDWARD VII PENINSULA

MT. HELEN WASHINGTON

ALEXANDRA MTS.

Cape Colbeck

ROCKEFELLER MTS.

Ross

Miles

0   200

Ross

Sea

Kainan Bay

ROOSEVELT I.

LITTLE AMERICA

Ice

75°   80°   85°

Shelf.

140°   150°   160°

Marie Byrd Land

On his second flight Ronne decided to follow the ice front all the way to Vahsel Bay, thus filling in the last stretch of unknown coast in this sector of Antarctica. Unfortunately, after he had flown for 450 miles along the ice cliffs, a cloud bank prevented him from covering the last ninety miles to Vahsel Bay. He flew forty miles inland and found, according to his radar altimeter, that the surface of the ice sheet rose 600 feet in that distance. This indicated that the ice was resting on land, and, combined with the results of the previous flight, proved, Ronne felt, that no strait could possibly cut Antarctica in two.

Eleven days later Ronne made the third and last important flight of his expedition, landing twice in virgin territory, where he was able to take sun sights and pin down his flight line—a boon to mapmakers trying to make use of his photographs. One of the landings was on the Ellsworth Highland eighty miles south of the Pacific coast. The other was on the icy crown of Charcot Island.

The Ronne expedition left in February, 1948. Some geographers felt that it had been a model operation, if only for the eighty-six aircraft landings in the field—half of them in virgin territory without prior ground reconnaissance—which enabled Ronne to take sun sights at his leisure and plot accurate flight tracks. Isaiah Bowman, president emeritus of Johns Hopkins University, wrote that Ronne, despite his small budget, "was able to return with a harvest of scientific findings that would be a credit to a far costlier expedition."

The British base at Stonington Island remained for another two years, during which time a number of sledge journeys were made in the Palmer Peninsula area under the leadership of Vivian E. Fuchs, a geologist who was later to head the British Transcontinental Party of 1957–1958.

Meanwhile both Argentina and Chile had opened a number of new outposts on Palmer Peninsula and its neighboring archipelagos. The Argentines carried out comparatively little exploration on land, but the Argentine navy did valuable work in placing aids to navigation and in charting.

There was intense rivalry over the claims question. Each claimant has its own name for Palmer Peninsula, as it is known in the United States. The British call it Graham Land for a former First Lord of the Admiralty. To the Argentines it is San Martin Land, and to the Chileans it is O'Higgins Land—in both cases named for national heroes who helped free them from Spanish rule.

The rivalry reached its crisis in 1947 and 1948 when capital ships were brought to Antarctica for the first time. Argentina sent a navy task force to Deception Island to establish a base four miles across the bay from the British outpost. Britain immediately sent a cruiser and frigate to the scene which arrived shortly after the Argentine squadron had left.

Subsequently, both countries, together with Chile, agreed not to make displays of force in the Antarctic during the coming season, and this agreement has been renewed annually.

20

La Terre Adélie

FOR OVER one hundred years after Dumont D'Urville, in 1840, discovered Adélie Land and claimed it for France, no French expedition ventured to that part of Antarctica. When one finally set forth in 1948 it was unable to breach the pack. The following season the Frenchmen had better luck, and in January, 1950, reached Cape Découverte, where they established their base, Port Martin.

For three years the French made a succession of trail trips which covered most of the Adélie Land coast and penetrated into the interior. Adélie Land is by far the smallest of the claims in Antarctica—so much so that on the map it resembles a sliver more than a pie slice. It was found to be much like the region which Mawson had explored to the east, with no mountains or rock outcrops visible even at the deepest French penetration to the interior.

In October, 1950, Dr. Jean Sapin-Jaloustre, biologist of the first wintering party, made a discovery which later enabled his countrymen to spy on the strange mating and egg-hatching rituals of the Emperor penguin. Fifty miles west of Port Martin he found himself among a cluster of rocky islets off the low promontory of Point Géologie.

184

In wonder he gazed at a multitude of Emperor penguins standing on the frozen sea between the islets.

"The wind blows without respite at 100 to 150 kilometers per hour," Sapin-Jaloustre wrote. "The blizzard reduces visibility to a meter and lets loose a ceaseless bombardment of small ice fragments; man has difficulty breathing, is incapable of any effort, and is blinded in a minute by a mask of ice.... In these conditions ... the Emperor hatches his egg."

During the winter night which followed Sapin-Jaloustre's discovery, Jean Cendron, who had relieved him as expedition biologist, was anxious to visit the rookery and obtain some eggs.

When he reached Point Géologie, he was unable to find the rookery for some time. Then suddenly he heard a series of sharp, metallic cries at close hand and realized that what he had taken to be a broad flat rock in the sea ice was in fact a penguin "huddle." The "huddle" was about 100 yards in diameter and contained about 5,000 birds, packed together so that the bird in the rear rested his head between the shoulders of the two birds in front of him. It was clearly a device for keeping warm.

The Frenchmen were eager to study the breeding habits of the penguins, but this project had to be postponed until the following winter, when a hut could be built at the rookery.

The January following Cendron's visit a man at Port Martin raced into the hut at three-thirty in the morning shouting "Fire! Fire!"

The workshop was a curtain of flame. With their fire

extinguishers the Frenchmen drove it back momentarily, but as soon as the extinguishers had been exhausted the flames leaped back and marched forward rapidly. Bottles of chemicals exploded in the blaze, releasing noxious gases that burned the throats of the fire-fighters and half blinded them.

Wildly they wielded hammers and picks in an effort to demolish the narrow passageway linking the science wing with their living quarters, but the 70-knot gale drove the flames past them, under the floor, and smoke began rising from the floorboards throughout their barracks. Within an hour their station lay in steaming ruins. They could only guess at the cause of the fire. It was the fourth Antarctic camp to burn within six years.

Port Martin had to be evacuated by the relief ship which fortunately was on hand, but the French decided to go ahead with their plans to leave another wintering party at Point Géologie. The seven men there were the first to witness the complete cycle of an Emperor penguin rookery.

Because the Emperors disperse into the pack during the exploration season only a few of their rookeries have been discovered. The actual total is probably in the hundreds. When the Frenchmen set up their camp there was no clue that a rookery site lay close by. On March 10 the first two birds arrived, and soon a third hopped out of the water and waddled over to the pair. The newcomer lowered his head to his chest in the typical bow of the Emperor and the greeting was returned.

Two weeks later, there were 1,100 birds present and they were arriving at the rate of about 400 a day, trekking across the ice in long single files from the north and northwest.

Soon after arrival, the birds began the difficult task of selecting a partner for the coming season. The penguin, which may be well over three feet tall, first stands at attention with his or her beak pointed toward the sky, neck craning as though to hear a distant sound. After posturing thus for a few moments, the outside of each flipper is rubbed with the beak, followed by a lowering of the head to the chest and the taking of a deep breath, whereupon the bird begins his love song. This is a complex and rhythmical affair ending in a long sustained note. Once finished, the bird again reaches for the sky, and thus the ritual ends as it began. This is done over and over as the birds wander about looking for partners. The song of the female is clearly different from that of the male and one can soon learn to distinguish them.

Having found a possible spouse, each bird goes through the ritual several times before the knot is tied, so to speak. "Imagine this performance being carried out by hundreds, even thousands of birds," wrote Mario Marret, leader of the party, "... and you have some idea of the strange and unique ballet that took place constantly at this period...."

By April the ritual had taken on an added intensity, for the mating period was at hand. The plump birds stood chest to chest, and at the final thrust of the beak heavenward became absolutely rigid as though in ecstasy. Even when prodded by a man, they continued to remain motionless.

Between May 5 and 20 the eggs were laid. The French spent many frigid hours trying to catch a bird in the act of laying but were never successful. Apparently it is done at the darkest time of night, and it is assumed that the egg is laid directly onto the ice, whereupon the mother rolls it onto her feet and works it under the heavy rolls of fat on her lower abdomen. This area is rich in blood vessels to keep the egg warm. The egg is large—about four inches in diameter—and may weigh as much as a pound.

The father's first view of the egg is obviously a moment of ecstasy for both parents. Normally, when tucked under the parent's belly, the egg is completely covered. When the father shows up the next day, however, the mother goes into her song-and-bow routine, exposing the egg at the proper moment. The father goes through a similar ceremony and reaches over to touch the egg with his beak as though to reassure himself that it is real.

At length the mother lets the egg roll onto the ice, whereupon the father eagerly "dribbles" it with his beak until he can work it up onto his feet and into his own belly folds. The mother then joins up with other females and treks north over the ice toward the fishing grounds. She does not return until the father has hatched the egg.

The incubation period proved to be from sixty-two to sixty-four days, during which time the brooding males remained almost motionless, usually in a tight huddle. It had now been four months since the birds had eaten, although an enormous number of calories must have been burned up to keep both themselves and the eggs warm.

Two days in advance the chicks began to cry inside their eggs, and when they emerged their cries brought about a complete change in the atmosphere of the rookery. The Emperor penguin has an obsessive desire to cuddle a chick in his belly folds. If the parent unwisely lets the child slip out onto the ice, there is a mad scramble. The childless Emperors cast all dignity to the winds in their effort to scoop up the chick into their own tummy folds.

For several days the chicks are unable to stand, and for a long time are fed by regurgitation of a nourishing substance from the crop of the parents. The youngster is tucked into the stomach folds even when so large that only its head can be crammed into the sanctuary, leaving a great, fuzzy posterior exposed to view.

During the brooding period, the population of the rookery was 6,200, but when the mothers returned from their fishing trip it swelled to 13,000—by far the largest number of Emperor penguins ever seen in one place. The mothers timed their return to coincide with the hatching period so that they could aid in feeding their youngsters. To find their husbands in that crowd was a problem, and sometimes it took a full day. Since sound, rather than sight, is their chief means of recognition, the female would stand in front of a group of males and sing.

The males responded with song, and if there was no mutual recognition she would move on to another group. "At such times," wrote Marret, "the rookery is agog and there is an almost deafening noise of song and counter-song."

The mortality of the chicks was very great, and during gales the little fuzzy bodies were blown all over the landscape. The Emperor lays only one egg a year, so that his longevity must be great to sustain the species.

The following summer the Norwegian sealer *Tottan,* chartered by France, arrived to close down the outposts in Adélie Land. The expedition members could find satisfaction in many accomplishments. Adélie Land was the first Antarctic claim whose coastal areas had been mapped with some degree of accuracy, and a large amount of scientific data had been assembled. Before they left, hopeful that it would not be another 100 years before Frenchmen again visited Adélie Land, they set a bottle of rum on the table with four glasses and a bouquet of artificial flowers.

21

The Cruise of the *Atka*

AN ARRAY of programs for research and exploration in the Antarctic began to take shape in the summer of 1954. Their impetus was the International Geophysical Year of 1957–1958. It was hoped that simultaneous observations in all parts of the world during the I.G.Y. could throw new light on many problems of geophysics, such as the nature of the aurora, the origin of cosmic rays, and the laws governing weather patterns.

Special emphasis was to be placed on the Antarctic, for it is still the least known of regions. Scientists from all the major nations of the world, meeting in Rome, selected twenty-eight desirable I.G.Y. observation sites in the Antarctic area.

The United States agreed to establish three stations on the Antarctic mainland. One was to be at the Pole itself, where no man had ever wintered. Another was to be in Marie Byrd Land, and the third at Little America.

Thus was born the great expedition, later designated *Operation Deepfreeze,* which was to continue from 1954 into 1959.

To find out if the *Highjump* base at Little America could still be used and to search the coast for other base

191

sites, the U. S. Navy icebreaker *Atka* was ordered south in late 1954 on a lonely scouting mission.

I joined the ship in Wellington, New Zealand, in January, 1955. There was much talk on board as to what would be found at the Bay of Whales. Remembering that the two converging ice rivers were gradually compressing the entrance to the bay, we discussed the possibility that a section of ice shelf might have cracked off and gone to sea, carrying with it the Little America camps.

At 2:30 on the morning of January 14 the ship was off the frontal cliffs of the Ross Ice Shelf. The navigator, Lieutenant Commander Frank A. Woodke, had been unable to get a sun sight for some time, but he felt that the ship should be close to Discovery Inlet. Woodke looked at the ice cliffs through his binoculars, then scanned the radar screen, but no sign of the inlet entrance was to be seen.

He finally obtained a few fleeting glimpses of the sun and, when he had worked out his sights, admitted rather abashedly that they placed the ship ten miles "inland."

At length, as we steamed eastward, a huge, shallow indentation appeared in the line of the cliffs. No feature of this nature showed on the chart. The conviction grew as we skirted its edges that this must be what was left of the Bay of Whales.

Suddenly several poles were seen on the inland ice plateau, one with a propeller spinning on top of it. It was the electric generator from Byrd's original Little America camp. A helicopter took off and located Little America III, the 1940 camp, which also appeared to be intact. But there was no sign of Little America IV, the 1947 tent city of *Operation Highjump*. As Paul Siple had predicted, the entire western side of the bay had broken off and floated out as one or more icebergs.

Woodke's navigation had been right all along. The ship was, indeed, ten miles "inland," for that much had broken off. Discovery Inlet was gone. A section at least as large as New York State's Long Island had "calved" from the Ross Ice Shelf. The gigantic forces which we had seen doing battle in 1947 had resolved their struggle.

During the day I made a helicopter flight to establish whether or not the 1947 camp really was gone. As we approached the brink of the ice cliffs we saw a pipe sticking twenty feet out of the snow—the flagpole of our old camp. Nearby were two rows of tent poles protruding a few inches above the surface. One row was incomplete, breaking off abruptly at the brink of the cliff.

Out over the ocean we looked back and saw a dark object embedded in the face of the white precipice. It was an oil drum, and beneath it was a dark line that ran seven and a half feet below the brink. The line marked the snow level which had been on the surface eight years before. Nearby a tent hung clinging from the face of the cliff. Something which resembled a folded Army cot hung free from one of the tent floorbeams, casting its shadow on the powdery white face of the cliff. A torn fragment of red cloth blew in the wind.

The camp had been cut in two as though by a gigantic meat cleaver. The other rows of tents, the operations hut, and the nine planes had vanished.

With the *Highjump* base cut in two, it could not be used for *Operation Deepfreeze,* and, without a harbor, the other installations at Little America were of little use, for they could be reached only by helicopter.

Another party was flown to Byrd's original camp and found that, after twenty-six years, the seventy-foot radio towers were almost completely buried. One protruded only a couple of inches, and I asked Commander Glen Jacobsen, the *Atka's* captain, to sit on it for a photograph. It was as if the fabulous tale of Baron von Munchausen, in which the snow was so deep that he hitched his horse to the tip of a church spire, had in effect come true.

While the *Atka* lay to off Little America, a helicopter flew a circuit of the bay area and found a great cleft in the ice shelf that ran eight miles southeast. The cleft seemed to indicate that another large section of the shelf was ready to break out. This final calving may sweep away what remains of the Little America camps, but at the same time the bay may again become useful as a harbor and remain free of major calving for another half century.

With the forty-four-year history of the Bay of Whales as one of the chief centers for Antarctic exploration at an end—or at least suspended—the *Atka* headed east to look for a substitute base site.

Her first destination was Sulzberger Bay, a great indentation 100 miles wide and 70 miles deep. It lay some 200 miles east of Little America, closer to the projected side of Byrd Station. It had never been entered by a ship, though several had come close to its entrance.

Almost within sight of Sulzberger Bay, the *Atka* encountered heavy pack extending up to the coast and was forced to turn back. Jacobsen then turned back to make a careful examination of Kainan Bay, thirty-five miles east of the original Little America. To test the ice-sheet surface and see if it could be compressed into a hard runway, several men were lifted onto the shelf by helicopter.

On the morning of January 22, 1955, I was below in the observers' living compartment when Tilghman, a helicopter flier, suddenly rushed into the darkened corner which I shared with the pilots and seized his flight clothes.

"There's been a crash," he said.

I ran up on deck and learned it was John Moore who had gone down. Within a few minutes we heard the pulsing beat of a helicopter in flight. It was coming in with Moore.

As the helicopter lowered onto the ice, I realized that we were immersed in a typical Antarctic white-out. Moore was quickly carried across the snow and up the gangway. We could not see his face, but his hand moved gently, so we knew he was alive.

From those who saw the crash the story was gradually pieced together, though John Moore never lived to give his version of it. He had just brought the Reverend Daniel Linehan, S.J., director of the Boston College Observatory, to set off some explosives to determine the ice-sheet thickness and whether it was aground at this

195

point. Moore dropped the scientist-priest and then lifted his machine into the air to return to the ship. Imperceptibly a white-out situation had developed, and there was no horizon. He tilted his machine forward for horizontal flight, but instead of flying parallel to the earth he flew in a thirty-degree descent. The machine crashed into the ice sheet at full power and tumbled for about seventy-five yards before coming to a stop, its pontoons in the air and the rest of the machine a tangle of twisted piping, torn metal, and shattered sections of the cockpit blister.

Meanwhile another helicopter, piloted by Albert P. Metrolis, was coming in and saw a strange tangle below. He landed and, with the other men on the ice, ran to the crashed machine. They found Moore enmeshed in the wreckage, his face in the snow, and carefully pulled him out.

"Where am I?" he said.

"You are out in the field," Metrolis replied.

"What am I doing here?"

"You've had an airplane accident. I'm going to take you back to the ship. Do you understand?"

"Yes."

Metrolis placed Moore in a boat sled and lashed him to one pontoon of his helicopter. Father Linehan kneeled in the snow alongside the pontoon, praying as the rotors whipped over his head, until Metrolis signaled that he was ready for take-off.

The crash took place at 10:20 A.M. and fifteen minutes later Moore was aboard ship—a quicker rescue could hardly be imagined. The ship's doctor found he was in deep shock due to multiple internal and head injuries. For three hours he worked to try to save the twenty-six-year-old flier. Moore never fully recovered consciousness, and at last, in the early afternoon, the commanding officer's voice came over the loudspeaker: "I regret to say that Lieutenant John Moore who crashed on the ice has just passed away."

This latest accident meant that three postwar Navy expeditions to Antarctica had lost planes through white-out conditions, and these crashes had taken four lives. Whereas other expeditions in this period were stricken by a succession of disastrous fires, the Navy fliers had been brought to grief by a strange white Lorelei that seemed to appear with little or no warning.

At a meeting of the observers it was agreed that Kainan Bay could serve as a harbor for the main *Deepfreeze* base. This was, in fact, the site finally chosen for "Little America V." Its exploration had cost us one of our best men and, although we knew from the history of Antarctic exploration that the frontiers of knowledge were sometimes pushed back only with loss of life, to those on the *Atka* and to Moore's family in North Carolina it seemed a high price to pay.

After several attempts to reach the coast farther east, the *Atka* set her course for Cape Norvegia on the far side of the Weddell Sea. Meanwhile the scientists and observers aboard her were working on a number of projects which anticipated the program of the International Geophysical Year.

197

One of the most important of these was the continuous recording of cosmic rays. Many nuclear physicists believe the clue to the origin of cosmic rays may be found in the polar regions. The nature of the mechanism that creates the rays fires the imagination, for the energies of cosmic particles greatly exceed those resulting from an atomic explosion. The polar regions are significant because only there does the magnetic field of the earth approach the vertical, permitting the penetration of low-energy cosmic particles which in other regions tend to be deflected at high elevations.

The two types of recorder on the *Atka* made the first joint survey of cosmic rays that has ever extended from one polar region to the other. The observations with this apparatus began in 1954 aboard the Canadian ice-breaker *Labrador,* which circumnavigated North America, steaming through the Northwest Passage. The instruments were then shifted to the *Atka.* One apparatus detected incoming mesons and the other recorded neutrons, thus capturing simultaneously the two most important cosmic-ray components which reach the earth.

The objective was to determine the changes in intensity with movement toward and away from the geomagnetic poles. The variation according to latitude was dramatically demonstrated. The low-energy particles, which reach the earth in the form of neutrons, struck the recording device at the rate of 5,500 an hour near the Equator, but this almost doubled, to 10,000 an hour, by the time the ship reached Antarctic waters. High-energy particles, represented by mesons, increased only 10 percent with the same change in location.

The survey also showed that, as in the Arctic, the rate does not increase all the way to the geomagnetic pole. The neutron bombardment levels off about 1,900 miles from that point, and the meson rate does so even farther from the Pole. Perhaps the reason for this leveling off will be discovered when the observations of the I.G.Y. have been studied and correlated.

The rays that produced the particles bombarding the *Atka's* instruments had energies reckoned in billions of electric volts. Despite this tremendous energy, the particles are too minute to be considered in themselves a potential source of power. Their significance is as a clue to the tremendous and as yet mysterious nuclear activity in the universe.

In another project, the scientists on the *Atka* daily tacked down a sheet of sticky paper to catch dust in the remote regions visited. Analysis of the paper would show to what extent radioactive particles, thrust into the upper air by atomic explosions, had enveloped the earth.

Twice daily the *Atka* sent a weather balloon into the upper regions of the atmosphere. It carried a small carton of weather instruments and a tiny radio transmitter which broadcast the weather data as the balloon ascended.

The lowest temperature recorded was 120.3° below zero. This extreme cold was found, not over the polar ice sheet, but near the Equator, at an elevation of 10.8 miles. The temperature tends to be lower over the

Equator because the stratosphere is highest there. The air gets colder as altitude increases until the stratosphere is reached; then it levels off or begins to get warmer. Hence the region with the highest stratosphere tends to produce the coldest air.

The atmosphere plunged in polar night may be an exception, particularly over the South Polar Plateau. There, during the six-month darkness, perhaps the coldest air of all is formed. The lowest temperature recorded by the expedition over Antarctica was 76° below zero at a height of 5.6 miles—44° warmer than the air over the Equator. However, this was in February, in the midst of the southern summer.

As the *Atka* passed through the equatorial regions, one of its balloons rose twelve miles above the sea before it entered the stratosphere. From the equator the height of the stratosphere sloped down toward the Pole, until in Antarctica it was found to be as low as three miles. Earlier observations at Little America suggest that in winter the stratosphere may sink right down onto the Polar Plateau, snuffing out the troposphere in which we live. Like the question of how cold it gets there during the winter night, this should be proved or disproved by the little group of Americans who are living there during the I.G.Y.

During its Antarctic cruise, the *Atka* "mailed" 2,500 letters by throwing them overboard. Each was a postcard sealed into a transparent, waterproof envelope, addressed to the U. S. Fish and Wildlife Service, Ann Arbor, Michigan. The finder was asked to jot down where and when it was found and drop it into the mail. The purpose was to find out where the waters flow from various points in the southern ocean. Little is known of currents in that area.

A large proportion of the cards were tossed over the side while the ship was crossing and recrossing the Antarctic Convergence. This is where the frigid seas of Antarctica meet the warmer waters of the Atlantic, Pacific, and Indian Oceans. Because of currents not yet fully understood, the change in temperature is sudden and marked. This sharp, but invisible, line means life or death to myriad tiny sea creatures—and to the great whales that pursue them. Even the sea birds know where it lies.

The *Atka* was especially equipped for oceanographic work of many sorts. At two dozen points off Antarctica, the "hydro team" hoisted a slim, rocket-shaped device over the side and let it plunge a mile or more to the bottom, where it scooped up a cross section of the sediment.

Every four hours the *Atka* lowered a series of sampling bottles into the water. Each had a built-in thermometer and was set to open at various depths. The water was thus tested at sixteen different layers for temperature and saltiness. Samples were also taken to be examined for heavy water (deuterium oxide) in connection with a worldwide survey of that substance, which provides the fuel for hydrogen bombs.

At every opportunity the *Atka's* oceanographer tossed his plankton net over the side and let it lie for a while a few-score feet down. It was like an elongated butterfly net, made of the finest gauzelike material, tapering to a cup at the end. The gentle current past the ship carried countless forms of drifting life into the net—some of them so tiny that they escaped even through the close-knit fabric. When at last he hauled it up, allowing the contents to settle into the cup, he carried into his laboratory a tumblerful of murky, greenish-brown water alive with little creatures of countless sorts. Under the microscope the variety of creatures was so great that every cubic centimeter was an entire aquarium. There were tiny shrimp-like crustaceans—the krill sifted from the water by whales—plus countless types of diatom, algae, jellyfish, and so forth.

The mission of the *Atka* on the Atlantic side of Antarctica was to find a site where an emergency air strip could be laid out on the continental ice sheet. This could provide an alternate field for planes of *Operation Deepfreeze* which were to lay down and supply the South Pole station.

The area which we were to examine was the coast of Queen Maud Land and a small portion of the east coast of the Weddell Sea.

The *Atka* scouted along the latter region, but was able to find only one likely-looking bay. Its waters were still partly frozen. Here several groups of Emperor penguins were sleeping on their bellies, and a hunting party was landed.

Aroused from their slumber the Emperors stood up and, stretching to their full three-foot height, glared at the intruders. As a sailor stalked his game the hunted penguin would begin to walk away, keeping a wary eye over his shoulder. The walk would break into a waddling run, and soon both sailor and bird were sprinting across the ice.

When the sailor got too close the bird would flop on its belly and toboggan much faster than a man could run. The trick was to lunge and tackle the bird before it did so. Then both sailor and penguin would slide another twenty yards while the penguin audience, never having seen a two-legged enemy, watched in bewilderment. It was a sight to gladden the heart of any football coach.

In all, six birds were captured and hoisted aboard feet first.

No satisfactory site was found in the bay, and the ship turned back to look east of Cape Norvegia. On February 16 we entered Norsel Bay, the harbor used by the Norwegian-British-Swedish Expedition. Here we perceived a strange phenomenon. Puffs of what looked like steam shot up from the face of the ice cliffs. It was not until we sailed in close that we saw the explanation. A side current of considerable force had eaten in under the cliffs at the water line, creating immense caverns of ice. Periodically a slight swell filled these with water, forcing out a blast of air which blew clouds of snow off the face of the cliff.

It was with a feeling of horror that the significance of these caverns dawned upon us, for it was here, four years earlier, that a weasel from Maudheim went over the ice cliff in a fog when a section of the "dock" had unexpectedly broken out. The four occupants saw the water and jumped, but too late.

Three of them—Ekström, a Swede, Jelbart, an Australian, and Quar, an Englishman—swam to the ice front and clung to it with their fingers, but the current sucked them into the caverns. The fourth man, Hallgren, pulled himself onto a floe with his sheath knife and saw his companions go under, one by one. Quar cried to Ekström, "Goodbye, Knalle!" before he vanished. Hallgren was finally saved.

Following the coast eastward, the *Atka* found a large bay twenty miles wide at its mouth and ten miles deep. What was most remarkable about this feature, now known as Atka Bay, was the uniform low level of the ice sheet along much of the southern shore. Being only fifteen feet high, it provided a dock where cargo could be unloaded and hauled directly to a base camp. Another, and even better site was found farther east, where a long tongue of continental ice pushed out into the sea. This proved to be so ideal a harbor that it was felt this discovery alone had made the trip worthwhile. The bay was almost five miles deep, tapering until at its end there was just room for about three ships to moor. The ice front was only six feet high—an ideal dock—and there were no cliffs barring access to the hinterland. In all directions from the head of the bay the surface sloped up to the plateau in gentle contours. Since there was no record of a previous landing in this area, Commander Jacobsen suggested that this be designated "Admiral Byrd Bay."

The survey of Byrd Bay was completed in a single day,

and the *Atka* headed homeward, setting her course for Buenos Aires.

En route the sailors struggled to keep alive eleven penguins which had been captured during the trip. They were to be donated to the National Zoological Park in Washington, D.C., and to the Bronx Zoo. Penguins are particularly hard to keep in captivity, as they almost invariably fall victim to aspergillosis, a fungus infection.

For the first few days it took four men an hour and a half to feed each bird: one man on each flipperlike wing, while a third pried the gullet open and the fourth shoved a strip of raw fish down the gullet. Then the bird's throat was stroked until it swallowed. Massive doses of vitamin pills were mixed with the fish to make up for the imbalance of the diet.

One of the chief concerns of the penguin keepers was the birds' refusal to drink. Living in a world where fresh water in the liquid state is almost unknown, they did not touch it. Great blocks of snow were brought aboard to be parceled out to the birds, and when this ran out the crew gave up its favorite dessert so that the ice cream machine could be used to make ice for the penguins.

As the *Atka* steamed through the warm waters off Argentina, the penguin keepers did all they could to keep their charges comfortable. A fire nozzle was rigged over their wading tank and the birds seemed to love it. The big Emperors laboriously climbed into the tank and waited their turn to stand under the shower, craning their necks upward and lifting their wings to let the water get under them in startlingly human fashion.

From Buenos Aires the penguins were flown to the United States. Unfortunately, they all died within a few months, except two that went to the Bronx Zoo.

During her six weeks in Antarctic waters, the *Atka* had girdled half the continent, sailing 7,500 miles. Her observer teams had landed at five points, four of them never before visited by man. She had made known the disappearance of the Bay of Whales, had found Kainan Bay suitable as a substitute and had discovered, at Byrd Bay, one of the most perfect harbors and base sites on the Antarctic coast. The *Atka's* scientists had brought home new knowledge of the air, water, snow, ice, and ocean floor at the bottom of the world, and of the regions of outer space that girdle the earth. Above all, the foundations had been laid for the much greater venture to come: *Operation Deepfreeze.*

22

The I.G.Y. Expeditions

THE International Geophysical Year was to be the first attempt by the scientists of the world to work together as a team in a study of our planet as a whole—its weather, its brittle crust, its molten heart and the space around it. In planning this great effort it was noted that scientific stations from which observations could be made were already scattered over most of the globe. There was but one great blank area—the Antarctic—and hence ten nations sent expeditions forth to fill in the gaps at the bottom of the world. Some of them, like Australia, Argentina, Britain, and Chile, already had stations there. The rest—France, Japan, New Zealand, Norway, the Soviet Union, and the United States—had to set up new bases.

By December of 1955 thirteen ships were converging on Antarctica bearing men from many lands. History's greatest assault on that continent had begun, and when it was over it was likely that most of the blank area on the world's maps would be filled in and the exhilarating experience of discovering new lands might be brought to an end.

The largest of these ventures was America's *Operation Deepfreeze*. Seven ships and about 1,800 men were engaged for the first season. As on *Highjump,* Admiral Byrd was "officer in charge" of the over-all project. Rear Admiral George Dufek, who had commanded the Eastern Group on *Highjump,* was in actual command of the naval units assigned the task of building stations for the scientists.

The new icebreaker, *Glacier,* more powerful by far than any of her predecessors, reached McMurdo Sound, site of Scott's old base, on December 17, 1955. The ice covering the frozen-over sound was tested with a chain saw, which cut down seven feet before breaking out into open water.

This seemed thick enough to carry the weight of four-engined ski planes, and three days later eight aircraft took off from New Zealand, 2,250 miles to the north. Six of the expedition ships were strung out along the route of this memorable flight to report weather, act as radio beacons, and make rescues in case of disaster. Two P2V Neptune patrol bombers and two four-engined Douglas transports (known on the airlines as Skymasters) completed the hop, but strong headwinds forced the four other smaller planes to turn back. The Neptunes carried a combination ski-wheel landing gear similar to that used on *Highjump.* The Douglas transports landed with wheels on the slippery ice. It was a delicate business, but the pilots set down their thirty-six-ton aircraft without mishap.

The four big planes were launched on a series of nine major flights which, for the first time, crisscrossed the heart of Antarctica, passing close to "The Pole of Inaccessibility"—that point which, in all directions, is farthest from the sea. The chances that some great mountain range, higher than the Himalayas, might lie hidden in the hinterland, or that—as Byrd once suggested—there might be a snow-free region, like the hot springs area of Iceland, were greatly reduced. As had been suspected from shallower penetrations by earlier expeditions, the center of Antarctica was a featureless ice plateau whose crest some pilots estimated at over 14,000 feet. This was so high that, on those flights on which the planes did not have oxygen, they could fly at only 500 feet above the surface, greatly reducing their range of vision.

The flights were crowded into a single spell of good weather from the third to the fourteenth of January, 1956, and were carried out under great handicaps. There were virtually no installations at the "airport," and to refill their gas tanks the planes usually had to taxi over to the tanker *Nespelen,* which laid out a fuel line on the ice.

Two of the flights crossed the continent. One of these, carrying Commander Hawkes, who headed the air unit at Little America on *Highjump,* flew directly to Vincennes Bay on the Knox Coast and then scouted for 120 miles along the shoreline. The other transcontinental flight, also with Hawkes aboard, reached the vicinity of the Weddell Sea, although that body of water was not actually seen. The plane, in general, followed the route of a transcontinental tractor trip projected by the British. Covering 3,450 miles in nineteen hours, this was the longest and probably the most interesting of the flights, for it crossed the region south of the Weddell Sea, hitherto the least known of Antarctica's coastal areas, and revealed four mountain ranges between the Pole and that sea—a discovery which presumably will greatly complicate the British program. The peaks ranged up to 10,000 feet, the fliers said, and lay in the 450-mile stretch between 85° South and the coast.

By the time this flight returned on January 14, a spell of warm weather had made the ice surface slushy—a poor runway for the big Skymaster wheels and a threat to all four aircraft, since the ice was likely to break up with the first storm. Dufek, therefore, called a halt to the exploration flights which, in nine hops, had covered a total of about 23,000 miles, and, on January 18, the planes flew back to New Zealand.

Meanwhile the expedition cargo ships were unloading supplies for two major bases on the coast. When they departed, in the early months of 1956, they left 166 men at elaborate camps which had been set up at McMurdo Sound and at Little America V, built a few miles south of Kainan Bay. Stored alongside the base at McMurdo were 500 tons of supplies to be parachuted, the next season, to establish an outpost at the South Pole. Likewise at Little America was a stockpile of hut panels, stoves, electric generators, and countless other items needed for another outpost to be placed by tractor train in the heart of Marie Byrd Land.

During the winter night, in temperatures that ranged even lower than 60° below zero, the men worked in preparation, packing parachute bundles, smoothing out

a runway on the ice, and so forth.   There were many set-
backs, but when the big planes returned from New Zealand in October of 1956, all was ready.   On the last day
of that month a ski-equipped, twin-engine Douglas transport, piloted by Lieutenant Commander Conrad S. Shinn,
landed at the South Pole.   The door opened and down
climbed Admiral Dufek, the first man to set foot at the
bottom of the world since Scott's brokenhearted party
started on its fatal return march.

The cold hit Dufek and his companions like an electric shock.   Having left the spring weather of New Zealand only a short time before, they found the temperature
of 58° below paralyzing.

The extreme cold impaired the plane's lubrication system, and there was a question whether or not it could
get into the air again.   Overhead a huge Air Force C-124
Globemaster with Major Cicero J. Ellen at the controls
and myself among those aboard, circled, ready to drop
emergency supplies in case those below were stranded.

"The nicest part of the whole flight," said "Gus" Shinn
afterward, "was Major Ellen with his big old monster
floating around above us the whole time."

After Dufek had unfurled the Stars and Stripes, he
and his companions climbed aboard and Shinn opened
his throttles wide.   Nothing happened.   The plane was
frozen to the surface.   He opened four jato bottles, which
sent four jet streams firing astern.   The plane shook vio-
lently, but did not move.   He opened four more bottles
and, with clouds of smoke enveloping the aircraft, it be-

gan to inch forward. Finally, with all fifteen jato bottles open, it took off and mushed along at a meager sixty miles an hour.

Fear had seized those overhead, for we could see nothing but smoke. In the cockpit of the crippled plane Shinn could hear Ellen's anxious voice on the radio: "Hey Gus, are you there? Are you there, Gus?" but for some moments Shinn was too busy to reply.

The plane returned safely to McMurdo, and for three weeks Dufek delayed the landing of a construction crew at the Pole until the weather had warmed a bit. Then the twin-engined transports returned, this time with eight men and a dogteam on board. After being landed the party, under Lieutenant Richard A. Bowers, took careful sights of the sun and determined that the actual position of the Pole was eight miles away. They thus arrived at their destination just as Amundsen had done forty-five years earlier—behind a dogteam.

More builders were landed, and the Air Force Globemasters, operating from the ice strip on McMurdo Sound, began parachuting prefabricated buildings and stockpiles of fuel and food, plus a tractor and a weasel to use in rounding up the windblown supplies. One bundle of girders blew over the horizon, and it took a full day to recover it.

Meanwhile a trail party had set out from Little America to try to lay out a safe highway for the 630-mile journey to the site designated for Byrd Station, deep in Marie Byrd Land. An attempt made the previous season had cost the life of one of the expedition's most experienced

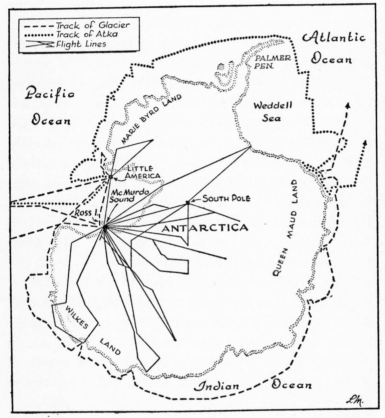

Tracks of Atka *and* Glacier *and flight lines from McMurdo Sound,* Operation Deepfreeze

tractor drivers, Max Kiel. His huge, thirty-seven-ton vehicle had broken through the snow bridge of a hidden crevasse. Two other men, during the first two seasons of *Deepfreeze,* were lost when their vehicles broke through the ice of McMurdo Sound.

An Army team, experienced in laying tractor trails across the Greenland ice cap, came down to blaze the trail to Byrd Station. With them they brought a newly developed crevasse detector. It consisted of seven large basins—like dishpans—five mounted on booms ahead of a weasel and two dragged behind. Electric impulses were sent through the ice between these basins. When there was a drop in current it was an indication of hidden air space below—a crevasse.

The device worked well, though it could not be depended on completely. The chief problem was to cross the region where the ice sheet slipped off the continent and became waterborne. Here, scouting ahead by helicopter, the trail men found a maze of crevasses. They were bridged with snow and often invisible from the surface. The helicopter landed lightly where these hidden pitfalls were sighted and someone leaned out to jab a warning flag into the snow. The pilot kept his rotors whipping hard, for sometimes the snow dropped out from under his wheels into a black abyss.

The trail blazers used up explosives at the rate of 800 pounds a mile in this area. Sticks of dynamite were set off wherever the crevasse detector gave a warning, and sometimes the snow would fall away into a hole big enough to hold an office building.

I spent ten days with this group, sleeping in a box which had been built on a sled. There were four shelves in the box, each long enough for one of us to lay out our sleeping bag. Though unheated, this "wannigan," as the lumbermen of the North Woods call it, was very comfortable. Meals were served in a Messing Wannigan, which was a small house on skis. What a contrast to the days of Scott! We were moving across a vast white prairie where no man had set foot before, but the man whose turn it was to cook rode in the wannigan, preparing the meal as we traveled.

With the completion of this trail a series of heavy tractor trains set forth along it, and before the season was out Byrd Station was manned and operating. Although deep in the heart of the continent, the residents of this outpost had many of the comforts of home. Like the men at the Pole itself, they were outfitted with washing machines, clothes driers, and "hi-fi" sets.

The U. S. Navy also set up stations at Cape Hallett, at Clark Peninsula on the coast of Wilkes Land, and in the Weddell Sea. The station at Cape Hallett was established only after a seesaw struggle with an army of about 150,000 penguins. The birds occupied the only suitable site. After a small area had been fenced off several thousand penguins were removed from within the enclosure by sailors and scientists, carrying baskets and boxes full of penguins.

Almost immediately, as though some penguin deity were taking revenge on the intruders, a storm drove ice fields down on the ships. The hull of the attack cargo ship *Arneb* was badly holed and the icebreaker *Northwind* lost a screw blade. Furthermore, when the air cleared, the men on board discovered that their fence was down and all the penguins had returned. The displacement of birds had to be repeated.

The *Arneb* escaped only to be further damaged in trying to reach Vincennes Bay, where Wilkes Station was to be established. By the end of the operation three-quarters of her ribs had been broken or badly bent and hoses over the side constantly gushed with water pumped from her leaky hull.

The ships in the Weddell Sea had an even harder time. They fought through the ice for a month, sailing almost to the southwest corner of that treacherous region of crushing pack—far beyond any earlier ships—but had to turn back and place their station near that of Argentina on the Filchner ice shelf. Ronne was left in command of the wintering party.

Meanwhile other expeditions were establishing themselves on the continent. British scientists set up a base on the east coast of the Weddell Sea. A more spectacular British venture was to be an attempt, in 1957–1958, to cross the continent by tractor, starting from the Weddell Sea and going, via the South Pole, to McMurdo Sound. It was to be an expedition in the spirit of Scott and Shackleton. A New Zealand party, headed by Sir Edmund Hillary, the conqueror of Mount Everest, would lay depots from McMurdo toward the British party, under

Vivian Fuchs, which was to start from the opposite side of Antarctica.

Apart from *Operation Deepfreeze,* the most elaborately equipped I.G.Y. expedition to head for Antarctica was that of the Soviet Union. It rode south in the *Ob,* a big 12,000-ton freighter especially designed for ice sailing, and another vessel, the *Lena.* The main base was built near Haswell Island and named Mirny for the Russian naval vessel which circled Antarctica more than a century before. There had been no Russian exploration in that area during the intervening years. The Soviet program called for establishment of stations at the Geomagnetic Pole, 900 miles inland, and at the Pole of Inaccessibility, 600 miles beyond that.

Early in 1956 the Russians made several flights to the hinterland and, by tractor train, set up "Pionerskaya Station" 230 miles out along the route to the Geomagnetic Pole.

Relations between the expeditions have been cordial. The Soviet and American outposts daily exchange weather information. There is a Soviet observer at Little America and an American at Mirny. By July 1, 1957, when the I.G.Y. officially got under way, ten nations had established about forty stations in various parts of Antarctica. Each was assigned specific fields of work—cosmic rays, aurora, weather, earthquakes, ice studies, and so forth. When the I.G.Y. is over the results will be assembled from all the expeditions and studied as a whole. In some cases it will be necessary to use elaborate business machines to

217

catalogue and analyze the tremendous volume of data.

Although the heroic tasks of geographical discovery in the Antarctic are fast vanishing, there will remain work for many generations of explorers which will accrue far more to the benefit of mankind than the sighting of new peaks and glaciers.

In 1932, J. Gordon Hayes, the Antarctic historian, wrote hopefully: "In future years, if human reason be supreme, adventures will occupy a more modest place in our esteem than the sober pursuit of truth." At last, with the International Geophysical Year, this prediction seems to be coming true.

At the same time, the I.G.Y., despite its purely scientific objectives, has political implications. In bringing to Antarctica the expeditions of many lands, including such political rivals as the United States and the Soviet Union, it underlines the necessity for finding a solution to the question of sovereignty over that area.

Claims to Antarctic territory have been made by seven nations: Argentina, Australia, Britain, Chile, France, New Zealand, and Norway. The United States has not made an official claim, but flags and claim sheets have been deposited by American expeditions.

Thus the situation stands today. Flags, claim sheets, and other emblems dropped from the planes of various nations lie congealed into the crust over the continent. Brass plaques look out over windswept mountains where men have visited but once. To those who have seen the vastness of the Antarctic ice sheet, the stark splendor of its mountains, the incredible fury of its winds, these displays of national rivalry around its fringes seem strangely absurd.

A movement has long been developing for international control of Antarctica. With the current parade of expeditions to that continent, the idea of such a solution is gaining ground. Edward Shackleton, son of the man who blazed the trail to the South Pole and an explorer in his own right, wrote in backing international rule: "We need not fear that we are betraying the great explorers of the past, for they sought nobler goals than the mere expansion of national territory."

The International Geophysical Year is in itself a step in the direction of international control. If it can be carried out without friction, despite rival ideologies, it will show that such a solution is feasible—a solution which, as Edward Shackleton said, would be appropriate to the ideals of the Antarctic heroes, whose epic feats are not likely to be repeated in an age of radio telephony, helicopters, and jet aircraft.

Index

MAJOR ANTARCTIC TREKS

1. First into the Hinterland, Scott, 1903
2. David's march to S. Magnetic Pole, 1908-09
3. Route to the Pole pioneered by Scott and Shackleton between 1902 & 1912
4. Amundsen's route to Geographic Pole, 1911-12
5. Bage's route to vicinity of S. Magnetic Pole, 1912-'13
6. Eastward march of Mawson, Mertz & Ninnis, 1912-'13
7. Gould, 1929-'30
8. Survey Party of U.S.A.S. 1940-'41
9. Ronne and Eklund, 1940-'41
10. Anglo-American Party, 1947-48
11. Norwegian-British-Swedish Expedition, 1951-'52
12. Soviet, 1956